William Allen White

Twayne's United States Authors Series

Kenneth Eble, Editor

University of Utah

TUSAS 441

WILLIAM ALLEN WHITE
(1868–1944)
*Photograph courtesy of
the Manuscript Division,
Library of Congress*

William Allen White

By E. Jay Jernigan

Eastern Michigan University

Twayne Publishers • *Boston*

William Allen White

E. Jay Jernigan

Book Production by Marne B. Sultz

Book Design by Barbara Anderson

Printed on permanent/durable acid-free
paper and bound in the United States of
America.

Library of Congress Cataloging in Publication Data

Jernigan, E. Jay, 1935–
    William Allen White.

    (Twayne's United States authors series; TUSAS 441)
    Bibliography: p. 144
    Includes index.
    1. White, William Allen, 1868–1944—Criticism and
interpretation. I. Title. II. Series.
PS3545.H617Z73   1983   818′.5209   83–6087
ISBN 0–8057–7380–0

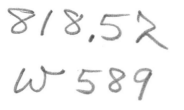
To Louise, Nathan, and David

Contents

About the Author

E. Jay Jernigan is a professor of English language and literature at Eastern Michigan University. He holds bachelor of arts and bachelor of science degrees from Kansas State Teachers College and master of arts and doctor of philosophy degrees from Kansas State University. He has taught at a high school, a junior college, and at several universities. In addition to his teaching, he has served since 1970 as an associate editor of the *Journal of Narrative Technique.* He has contributed the earlier volume *Henry Demarest Lloyd* to the Twayne United States Authors Series and has published in such journals as *Nineteenth Century Fiction, Michigan Academician, Kansas Quarterly,* and *Bulletin of the New York Public Library.*

Preface

Today we remember the Kansas newspaperman William Allen White as America's most prominent small-town editor and publicist of the first four decades of this century, one of the last of our independent personal journalists. But to his generation, and the one following, he was far more than the outspoken editor of the *Emporia Gazette*: he was an author of popular regional short stories, a novelist of promise, a leading Progressive Republican, a magazine free-lancer of authoritative political and social commentary, and an ebullient embodiment of moderately liberal Midwestern middle-class values. His career stretched over fifty-four years—from 1890, when he became assistant editor of the *El Dorado Republican*, to just before his death in 1944, when he dictated his last memo as publisher-editor of the *Gazette*. He first became known nationally in 1896 as the author of the sardonically Conservative Republican editorial "What's the Matter with Kansas?" which Mark Hanna used widely in his campaign to elect William McKinley president. Then in 1900 White signed on as an outside member of Samuel S. McClure's brilliant staff of magazine crusaders. Soon he became an unofficial advance man for Theodore Roosevelt, bolting with him in 1912 to form the Progressive party and remaining one of its leaders to the bitter end in 1916.

By 1920 he had rejoined the Republicans to raise a prophet's voice within the reactionary wilderness, winning a Pulitzer prize in 1923 for a *Gazette* editorial upholding freedom of speech in times of political stress. In 1924 he temporarily bolted his state party to run for governor of Kansas as an independent opposed to the Ku Klux Klan, the most visible force of postwar reaction. During the hard times of the 1930s he used his national identity as the "Sage of Emporia" to counsel political moderation in support of traditional decentralized democracy. Then in 1939–40, while in his seventies, he led two effective nonpartisan publicity movements to pressure Congress to back President Franklin D. Roosevelt's foreign policy of aiding the Allies, short of war. His posthumous autobiography, a bestseller, won for him in 1947 his second Pulitzer prize, a testimony to his contemporary stature as a national folk hero and journalist.

Because of that stature, White has evoked five book-length biographial studies, three of them substantial, scholarly works. But none discusses in any systematic way his numerous publications. Instead, those studies concentrate on his busy and often influential involvement in the Progressive Movement and Republican politics or on his career as a whimsically exuberant newspaper editor. Most scholarly journal articles about him focus upon some facet of his political influence. Yet during the first part of his career he was known as an author of fiction as much as a political journalist. And throughout his career he was a popular and versatile writer of interpretive articles and sketches for national magazines. At the present time interest continues in his various publications; for example, eleven of his books are still in print or available in reprint editions.

Consequently, the purpose of this study is to present for the first time a systematic analysis and critical assessment of William Allen White's voluminous publications. Yet that volume, in and of itself, poses a problem for the student of White. As a journalist he placed most of his work initially in newspapers, whose back files are virtually inaccessible, or magazines, whose prior volumes are not readily available. Fortunately for subsequent readers, he and others collected selections of that work and published them in book form. Of his twenty-five books sixteen are collections, in varying measure, of his short stories, editorials, magazine articles, syndicated newspaper copy, lectures, or letters. Thus in total his books are surprisingly representative of his written work. As a matter of simple practicality, then, I have concentrated on those books, though I also refer, when appropriate, to his uncollected works in order to convey his full range as a writer. I have not, however, analyzed his poetry per se, because it is negligible newspaper verse, nor have I discussed as such the two posthumous collections of his personal letters, because he did not write them for publication, though I do occasionally cite from them and from his unpublished letters to substantiate my commentary. Altogether, I have in this study analyzed twenty-one of his twenty-five books, my goal being to cover as much of his written work as possible within the bounds of this series and at the same time avoid, as much as possible, superficiality and banality.

In the two introductory chapters of this study I review White's life and times, a review designed to provide a biographical and historical perspective suitable for an informed critical analysis of his written work. That biographical unit is necessarily long because most of his

Preface

writings and activities concerned politics or current events. In chapter 3 I discuss first his qualities as a small-town editor, then analyze his journalistic work as revealed by six of his books based on that work. In chapter 4 I describe and analyze in chronological order his eight books of fiction. Chapter 5 covers his work as a "social historian" and concerns his several books of social analysis, his biographies, and his autobiography in that order. Then in a brief final chapter I discuss White's place in the thought of his time and assess his significance for his day and for ours.

In researching this study I have consulted the extensive William Allen White manuscript collections at the Library of Congress, Emporia State University, and the University of Kansas. The librarians whom I conferred with at those three institutions were universally kind, but I wish in particular to mention the helpfulness of Miss Mary E. Bogan, Special Collections Librarian at Emporia State. Likewise, staff members at the Graduate Library of the University of Michigan and at the Center for Educational Resources at Eastern Michigan University responded beyond perfunctory duty whenever I asked for aid. I wish also to express gratitude to my sister, Mrs. Evalee Williams, my mother, Mrs. Evelyn Jernigan, and a long-time family friend Mrs. Florence Feltner, each of whom gathered for my use miscellaneous materials about White and the *Emporia Gazette*; and I wish to thank Mrs. Kathrine (W. L.) White for her attention to my several requests for information and publishing permissions and Ms. Peg Crall for her bibliographical assistance. Here, too, I should like to commend two close friends from Emporia, Robert L. Morton and Billy G. Collins, for encouraging me during this project. My greatest scholarly debt in this study, as I indicate in my documentation, is to Walter Johnson's *William Allen White's America* (1947), the definitive biography, which is invaluable to any student of White or of American social history during his era; I am much obliged to Professor Johnson's work. I am also most grateful to Louise, my wife, who in addition to her own duties as a full-time university professor kept our two young sons from dropping peanut butter in my typewriter during the sabbatical term the regents of Eastern Michigan University granted me to complete this book.

E. Jay Jernigan

Eastern Michigan University

Acknowledgments

Permissions to quote copyrighted material, or material in which literary rights are reserved, are gratefully acknowledged as follows: from letters in the William Allen White collections at the Library of Congress and at the Spencer Research Library, University of Kansas, by permission of Mrs. William L. White; from *Masks in a Pageant*, copyright 1928 by Macmillan Publishing Co., Inc., reprinted by permission of Mrs. William L. White; from *The Autobiography of William Allen White*, copyright 1946 by Macmillan Publishing Co., Inc., renewed 1974 by Macmillan Publishing Co., Inc., and W. L. White; from *Woodrow Wilson: The Man, His Times and His Task*, by William Allen White, reprinted by permission of Houghton Mifflin Company; from *Selected Letters of William Allen White 1899–1943*, edited by Walter Johnson, copyright 1947 by Holt, Rinehart and Winston, reprinted by permission of Holt, Rinehart and Winston, Publishers, and by Walter Johnson; from *Forty Years on Main Street*, by William Allen White, compiled by Russell H. Fitzgibbon, copyright 1937 by William Allen White, copyright 1965 by Holt, Rinehart and Winston, reprinted by permission of Holt, Rinehart and Winston, Publishers.

Chronology

1921 Daughter dies from horse-riding accident; writes widely reprinted editorial tribute to her.

1922 Writes Pulitzer-prize-winning editorial "To an Anxious Friend" in defense of freedom of speech.

1924 *Woodrow Wilson.* Runs for governor of Kansas as independent against Ku Klux Klan.

1925 *Calvin Coolidge.*

1926–1944 Serves as one of five original Book-of-the-Month Club judges.

1928 *Masks in a Pageant.*

1930 Appointed to Haiti Commission.

1931 Appointed to President's Organization for Unemployment Relief.

1933 Covers London Economic Conference for North American Newspaper Alliance. Tours Europe for four months.

1935–1936 Inspects hospitals in Phillipines and China on behalf of Rockefeller Foundation.

1938 *A Puritan in Babylon.*

1939 *The Changing West.* Chairs Non-Partisan Committee for Peace through Revision of the Neutrality Act.

1940–1941 Chairs Committee to Defend America by Aiding the Allies.

1944 Dies in Emporia, Kansas, 29 January.

1946 Posthumous publication of Pulitzer-prize-winning *Autobiography.*

Chapter One

The Making of a Progressive: 1868 - 1916

Boy and Youth

William Allen White was born 10 February 1868 in Emporia, Kansas, the first and only surviving child of a middle-aged, temperamentally mismatched couple. His father, Dr. Allen White, forty-nine years old, was an Emporia physician and general store keeper, a staunch Copperhead Democrat, and a short, fat, easygoing humorist of colonial Yankee farming stock. His mother, Mary Ann Hatton White, thirty-eight years of age, was a former school teacher and an ardent Abolitionist Republican, slight of figure but hard-working, short-tempered, and totally humorless; she was second generation Irish orphaned early. Though she had taught two terms in nearby villages, "Old Doc" White met Miss Hatton but once, as a customer in his store, just before she left Kansas to stay with her married sister in Michigan. Smitten by her red hair and reports of her plucky spirit, he decided to court her by mail. After a short, awkwardly formal correspondence he journeyed to Michigan to marry her ten months before "Willie's" birth.[1]

Like this curiously makeshift courtship, Emporia too in 1867 had little time for the amenities, having been founded just ten years before. Set between the rich bottom lands of the Neosho and Cottonwood rivers in the bluestem grasslands of east-central Kansas, it was a slapdash but flourishing frontier town, the seat of Lyon County and the state normal college. Yet for Dr. Allen White, Emporia, with a population of nearly 800 in 1868, had become too settled. So the next year he sold his store and moved wife and son to El Dorado, a tiny village established only a year before on the Walnut River, sixty miles southwest. There he opened another general store and practiced medicine occasionally. Prominent in the successful fight to make El Dorado the seat of Butler County, he was one of the town's

leading citizens and eventually its mayor. His son was conscious
early in life that he was a member of the "ruling class."

But in the agrarian economy and rude democracy of the Kansas
frontier, "ruling class" was something of a misnomer. For the frontier
was essentially an egalitarian society in which anyone with gumption
considered himself middle class. As White was to remember El
Dorado, before the railroad came through, it was a self-sufficient
rural community, a preindustrial, Jeffersonian idyll. And that way of
life, even though its economic self-sufficiency soon passed away, served
as the ethical touchstone by which he judged all societies throughout
most of his life and in most of his works. As his one-time Emporia
friend the literary historian Vernon L. Parrington observed, two
major ideas were to dominate the mature White: "belief in the excellence of western village life" and "fear lest this life be submerged
by industrialism."[2]

In 1871 Mary Ann White bore another son, who died within a
year, so Willie grew up a favored only child but in rough and tumble
equality with the other children of the village, a childhood he celebrated later in a series of magazine short stories collected under the
title *The Court of Boyville* (1899). When Willie was five or six,
"Old Doc" tried to re-create his own youth by taking up farming in
pioneer style five miles northeast of El Dorado. But he soon returned
to town, where he built a large frame house with flamboyant verandas
and set it up as a hotel. After working his wife to a frazzle, he reluctantly gave up the hotel business when she fell ill and supported
his family comfortably by trading in real estate and keeping a few
boarders.

Though fussed over by his mother, Willie remembered his father
as strongly insistent that "the boy" not grow up coddled but do
chores and odd jobs and fight his own fights. Death took Allen White
and his immediate influence when Willie was only fourteen, but
throughout his adult life there was never doubt that he was his
father's son, having his short, portly physique and his key personality
traits of a buoyant optimism, a hyperbolic sense of humor, and an
exuberant gregariousness. Willie's mother, on the other hand, lived
until age ninety-four, dying when her "boy" was fifty-six; he once
described her as "the type of woman known as a 'captain'—a masterful person who had her own ideas."[3] She was to be one of the most
intimate and dominant forces in his life, keeping house for him until
he married, then living with or next door to him until her death. From

her he got his independent spirit and his love for books and music.

In May 1884 at the age of sixteen Will White graduated from El Dorado High School. That September he attended the College of Emporia, largely because it was near El Dorado, where his mother remained to keep boarders and look after their several rental properties. That college was a tiny Presbyterian school founded only two years before and holding classes for its less than 100 students on the third floor of a downtown business building. Will was unimpressed by its six faculty members and limited curriculum, but he did form an important, lifelong friendship with fellow student Vernon Kellogg, later a renowned professor of entomology and a respected war relief administrator, who whetted his interest in books and ideas. Will's boardinghouse roommates were working their ways through school, unlike him, which embarrassed his nascent sense of manhood, so he returned to El Dorado at the end of that school year determined to learn a trade to help support himself and allow his mother to give up boarders.

By chance he got a job as a printer's devil for the *Butler County Democrat,* a weekly whose shiftless editor still owed "Old Doc" several favors. Will worked there until the following December, learning to set type and to write in the florid style of small-town political journalism. Then he returned to the College of Emporia for the winter term and landed a job on the *Emporia Daily News.* That summer he returned home to work on State Senator Bent Murdock's *El Dorado Republican.* Murdock was a fatherly figure to Will White; he was a long-time family friend, who had boarded with the Whites, and one of the state Republican bosses on behalf of several local railroads and the Santa Fe. That fall, dissatisfied with the Emporia school, Will decided to follow Vernon Kellogg to Lawrence, Kansas, to enroll at the state university. His mother rented out the big house in El Dorado and moved with him.

Will attended the University of Kansas three and a half years where, as he observed later, he "got the habit of trained attention to the printed page" which "is about the best that any man gets out of a college education."[4] Under the tutelage of Vernon Kellogg he pledged Phi Delta Theta social fraternity and gradually established himself a leader in campus politics, becoming friends with a number of talented students with notable later careers, such as U.S. Army General Fred Funston, U.S. senator for Idaho William Borah, Missouri Governor Herbert Hadley, and the Stanford and MIT professors

Edward and William Franklin. While maintaining a "B" average in his course work, Will devoted much of his youthful exuberance to extracurricular matters. In addition to bossing campus politics, he contributed to and edited school publications, worked as a reporter for the *Lawrence Journal*, one of the two local dailies, and was Lawrence correspondent for the *St. Louis Globe-Democrat*, the *Kansas City News*, and the *El Dorado Republican*. One of his most salient traits throughout life was hustle; truly, he learned by doing. At the end of his third year he remembered spending "the most notable summer" of his life camping in an isolated area of the Colorado Rockies with a dozen other University of Kansas students, notable because he "learned to live with others" and because he fell in love with the Colorado mountains, where he was to spend parts of many later summers.[5] During the 1889 fall term, White realized he would not receive a degree because he continued to fail a required solid geometry course and had lost interest in his other class work. So he accepted an offer from Bent Murdock to take over the *El Dorado Republican* while he served on an important standing committee of the state senate. Will and his mother moved back to El Dorado.

Young Journalist

Other than to follow the Republican party line, White at twenty-two had virtually a free hand as assistant editor of the paper, an established country weekly with a circulation of almost 3,000. With youthful gusto he attended both to management and makeup, shoring up advertising accounts and churning out reams of copy, including free-lanced light general features and rural dialect verse in the manner of James Whitcomb Riley for a firm that sold them as "boilerplate" (ready-print stereotype plates) to small-town weeklies. White worked for Murdock nearly two years and from him learned how to write with controlled vigor and how to manipulate local politics.[6] But in 1890 Butler County politics were not responding very readily to Murdock's commands. The economic depression that was to spread world-wide by 1893 had already hit Kansas. Here rapid expansion and unwise speculation in the 1870s and early 1880s had created overweening public and private debts rendered inordinately burdensome in the late 1880s by drought and currency deflation. Its farmers and small businessmen were restive, no longer satisfied by GOP shibboleths and patronage. For them the common-law marriage of politics and Big Business had stopped being a joke; the Gilded Age had lost its glitter. Such economic unrest and political disillusion served as catalysts in 1892 for the national fusion of protestors in a strong third-party movement, the Populist or People's party. White experienced a preview of that fusion in 1890 when the Farmer's Alliance put up a state and county slate. At that time he was a neophyte gold-standard Republican and attacked the Alliance with editorial brashness, both out of conviction and to please Murdock. Consequently, he found himself hanged in effigy in an Alliance parade with "Silly Willy" emblazoned across exaggerated buttocks. He was now a somebody among local Republicans. But the Alliance won Butler County and captured the state legislature.

While political revolt seethed throughout Kansas during 1891, White happily served as Murdock's aide-de-camp, rallying the Old Guard editorially and bossing the county delegation to the Young Republican Convention at Topeka, the state capital. Soon after that convention he wrote his first piece of fiction, a blatantly sentimental tale about the return of a Civil War veteran to the Grand Old Party after his brief desertion to the Alliance. Headed "The Regeneration of Colonel Hucks," it helped fill the weekly demand for copy. To White's surprise, several Kansas dailies copied it on exchange, then the Republican state central committee sent it in boilerplate to all Kansas weeklies as part of its campaign against the insurgents. Maudlin and slight though it is, this story was momentous to his career because it gave him his first taste of more than local fame, which encouraged him to write further sketches, and it helped provide his ticket out of El Dorado. For it brought him to the attention of Colonel William R. Nelson, independently Democratic owner of the *Kansas City Star*, and to that of Charles S. Gleed, one of the directors of the Santa Fe Railroad which controlled the *Kansas City Journal*. Both offered him an editorial job, but he went with the *Journal*, an unwise but educational choice, for it introduced him to timid, machine-run journalism, which soon disgusted him.

Unsure about being able at twenty-three to hold a job with a big-city daily, especially in the midst of a deepening financial depression, he went alone to Kansas City, with his mother to join him when he felt established. After five months at the editorial desk, he requested transfer to Topeka as the Kansas political reporter, a more exciting position in his eyes because it was an election year. But within five more months, he quit the *Journal* in disgust when the telegraph editor timorously buried his scoop about the Populists' nominating a darkhorse for governor, a scoop that he had bragged about inordinately to fellow reporters. Luck was with him; one of Colonel Nelson's editorial writers quit just at that time, and White talked himself into a slot at the *Star*.

Under Nelson the *Star* in 1892 was a personal, crusading newspaper of unquestionable integrity and high standards. It supported Democrat Grover Cleveland nationally, but remained independent locally. With a daily circulation of over 50,000 it had become the dominant newspaper of the city and its Missouri and Kansas environs. It proved a dominant force in White's life too, for during his three years there he learned the ethics of a free press and what it meant to be an honest newspaperman. Then for over four decades as editor-publisher of a Kansas small-town daily, he often worked in tandem with the editorial staff of the *Star*, especially Henry J. Haskell and Roy A. Roberts, to pull for the same regional social and political policies. Though Nelson had hired him specifically to write "minion" editorials, light pieces of commentary that filled out the editorial page, he was given other editorial duties as well and assigned to reporting jobs occasionally, because the Colonel ran a loose but busy office. From a talented group of fellow editors—Noble Prentis, Tom Johnston, Alex Butts, and James Runyan, all older than he—White learned to get a hammerlock on his sometimes troublesome sense of humor and to tighten his style further.

During his first months in Kansas City, while working at the *Journal*, Will met a young, pretty school teacher named Sallie Lindsay. She was of genteel Kentucky stock, the oldest of ten children of a former Confederate cavalry captain, whose wife managed to keep their large family socially respectable on his modest salary as yard superintendent at one of the large meat packing plants in the Kansas City bottoms. Sallie became the love of White's life, his wife of more than fifty years, and the single-most beneficial influence upon his career. He soon learned to respect her as his intellectual equal, and grew to regard her as his most trustworthy confidant, advisor, and critic.[7] They were married 27 April 1893 in a family-only ceremony at the Lindsay's. He obtained a paid leave-of-absence from the *Star* and, using complimentary railroad passes, they left to honeymoon in New Mexico and Colorado. But in that year of financial panic they were nearly stranded in Colorado when the *Star* notified him, after he had unilaterally extended his leave, that because of retrenchment he was fired. A day after receiving that message, he and Sallie learned that a bank failure had wiped out their small savings account. Fortunately for them one of the *Star*'s senior editors fell ill a week later, and Managing Editor Johnston wired White he could have his job back if he returned immediately; he did.

Back in Kansas City, Will and Sallie set up housekeeping with his mother to cut down on expenses, and he held on to his job with the *Star* as a general purpose editorial writer and political reporter. Because of his inveterate sense of humor, though, his features were sometimes gratuitously flippant and offended advertisers or special interest groups, who protested loudly to Johnston. Later, when White was given the added assignment of writing minion features for the Sunday edition, he tried to keep out of further trouble by writing newspaper verse or homely fictional sketches with local backgrounds for feature copy. Since his university days he had fancied himself something of a poet. When he was with the *El Dorado Republican*, he had struck up a friendship with the young writer Albert Bigelow Paine, then living in Fort Scott, Kansas, and together they planned to publish a book of their poetry with a local printer. Those plans slowly took shape and in the late summer of 1893 *Rhymes by Two Friends* appeared. Unfortunately, the two friends had a misunderstanding about the distribution of review copies and ceased to be friends. Apparently, Sallie was not much impressed by Will's verse because, so he reported in his autobiography, she told him early in their marriage that prose was his true forte and encouraged his writing of fiction.

She also encouraged his dream of editing his own newspaper. Although Nelson was an easy boss and Kansas City offered the excitement of a fast-growing metropolitan area, Will was dissatisfied. He longed for independence and for the life of a small Kansas town. But he also wanted the stimuli of a college town, and that narrowed his choices considerably. His search for a paper was complicated too by lack of capital in the midst of continuing hard times. Nevertheless, he had tried to buy papers at Lawrence and Ottawa before he learned early in 1895 that the *Gazette*, one of the two small dailies in Emporia, might be for sale. After several months of negotiation, he bought it for $3,000, which he put together by borrowing from a local banker, from the estate of former U.S. Senator Preston B. Plumb, and from banker-governor Edmund Morrill. To do so he put up his mother's properties in El Dorado and used the influence of Cy Leland, a family friend from El Dorado and state Republican boss at this time. On Saturday, 1 June 1895, William Allen White stepped off the afternoon train from Kansas City, the twenty-seven-year-old owner of a small-town daily, a man who had but $1.25 in his pocket and had left his wife and mother in Kansas City to follow when he could afford it. He was now his own editor but his mortgages identified him with one of the two bank factions in town and with the conservative wing of the state Republican Party, which he also supported out of conviction.

Small-Town Editor

In his introductory editorial for Monday, Will announced his aims, which remained essentially the same the rest of his life. He wanted to make Emporia his hometown and be proud to be "from Emporia"; he wanted to reflect the sentiment of the "best" people in town (later, he admitted "I know now that there is no group of best people"); and he wanted to run a clean, honest Republican newspaper in which politics would be limited to the editorial page and the editor would never seek office. Last and most significant, he announced, "I shall hustle advertising, job work and subscriptions, and write editorials and 'telegraph' twelve hours a day in spite of my ideals. The path of glory is barred hog tight for the man who does not labor while he waits."[8] The *Gazette* had a circulation of less than 600 when he took over, and his chief competitor, former Lieutenant Governor Charles V. Eskridge, noticed his arrival in the *Emporia Republican* the following Tuesday with a condescending welcome in which he implied that White's failure was but a matter of time. That first year failure did indeed seem imminent, because each Friday he had to cover the payroll with a bank overdraft that lingered on through much of the next week. But hard work and long hours from both Will and Sallie, dedication from their small staff, and the good luck of receiving the town's printing contract when his bank faction captured local politics helped put the paper on its feet. Within a year it had outstripped the *Republican*, and within ten years that daily was the one which closed its doors. During the last thirty-nine years of White's life the *Gazette* had only a small Democratic weekly, the *Emporia Times*, as a persistent but insignificant competitor, though the rival Republican faction in town did start up another daily which lasted less than two years, during 1909–10.[9]

Of course, much of White's success was due to his ever-lasting hustle. As he remarked in the *Autobiography*, "I believed that local news, if honestly and energetically presented, would do more for the *Gazette*'s standing in the community than its editorial page." So he emphasized community news and covered the courthouse and city offices thoroughly, rather than respond to the editorial attacks that occurred from time to time in the *Republican.* Sallie contributed by covering local society news. Thus White remembered, "We stressed local news and printed a number of items that ordinarily would not have been printed in a strictly conventional newspaper. We were chatty, colloquial, incisive, impertinent, ribald, and enterprising in our treatment of local events. . . . Circulation grew" (269). Soon he contracted for the AP morning telegraph bulletin instead of relying for state and national news on the previous evening's *Kansas City Star* or on other day-old newspaper exchanges.

As filler during his first months at the *Gazette*, he printed several of his short stories rejected earlier by the Sunday editor of the *Star.* Those stories were copied by other newspapers and during the winter of 1895–96 elicited letters from two publishers, Way and Williams of Chicago, and Henry Holt of New York, asking if he had enough other stories like them to make up a book. Flattered, he and Sallie selected among those he had written for the *El Dorado Republican* and the *Star*, revised them extensively, added several new ones, then sent their selection to Way and Williams because it was a "western" firm. That firm published the collection under the title *The Real Issue* late in the fall of 1896, after White had received nation-wide notoriety from an editorial he wrote that summer for the *Gazette.* Headed "What's the Matter with Kansas?" that editorial had more influence on his life than anything else he ever wrote. Here is how it happened.

The year 1896 was a turbulent election year because the free silver advocates and the Populists were at the height of their rebellions. In June White grabbed an offer from the *Kansas City World* to report the Republican convention at St. Louis; it was his first trip "back East." There he sampled German restaurants with Ed Howe, novelist and crusty editor of the *Atchinson Daily Globe*, and with him followed the intrigues of the convention, especially those of Ohio Senator Mark Hanna, the Republican national boss who engineered the nomination of William McKinley on an outright gold plank. White admired Hanna's deportment and policy, viewing him from a conventionally conservative Republican stance. When Will returned home, he found Sallie ill, and on her doctor's advice took her to Colorado to stay with his Aunt Kate, who was running a small hotel there. He returned home the first part of July, in time to catch the telegraph report of William Jennings Bryan's nomination by the Democrats in Chicago on a free silver platform, and the report a week later from St. Louis of the fusion of the Populists with the Democrats in support of Bryan. He regarded Bryan as an unconscionable demagogue appealing to discontented rabble.

It was very hot in Emporia the rest of that summer, and for White the heat was from more than weather. At that time he was an outspoken, standpat gold-standard Republican running a newspaper in a depressed rural community that had gone Populist in 1892 and 1894 and would again in 1896. In fact, his newspaper had originally been started in 1890 expressly to support the Farmer's Alliance. Understandably, then, local Populists resurrected the epithet "Silly Willy" for an effigy in their processions and often baited White when he appeared on the streets. Thus, he looked forward to late Saturday afternoon, 15 August, when he could escape for a week by catching the Santa Fe to Colorado. He had just received the first set of proofs of his short story collection from Way and Williams and was excitedly anticipating going over them with Sallie.[10] But that morning on his way back from the post office a handful of farmers come to town for Saturday marketday badgered him about his editorial stance. As White reported the incident in the third person thirty years later, "somehow his language got jammed. The madder he got the more he sputtered and the less he spoke, and his face lost all expression except its color. He looked as featureless and as mad as a freshly spanked baby in the combat area, and finally, with his arms full of mail, stalked proudly down the street with a number of thoughts corked up in him."[11] When he got back to his desk, he was still mad clean through and remembered a conversation he had earlier that summer with Eugene Ware, conservative Republican lawyer and quondam poet, in which Ware held the Populists up to scorn for "ruining" the state and cited facts and figures to support his case. Using some of Ware's material, White poured out his wrath upon the Populists in a vitriolically satiric editorial which he slammed on the copy hook for that evening's edition, then finished his other duties and boarded the train.

Recalling those events in a 1904 editorial, White acknowledged,

" 'What's the Matter with Kansas' was a scratch shot. It couldn't be duplicated. There wasn't an original idea or expression in the whole piece; it was merely what had been heard on the streets, in offices and on trains. It was a mirror of the popular temper at that time. But it brought lots of luck. . . ."[12] Paul Morton, at that time vice-president of the Santa Fe, read it by chance and recommended it to Herman Kohlsaat, publisher of the *Chicago Times-Herald* and *Evening Post*, who reprinted it in both papers. Then the *New York Sun* picked it up, whereby it came to the attention of Mark Hanna, who as chairman of the Republican National Committee distributed it as a campaign pamphlet. It was soon reprinted in nearly every sizcable Republican newspaper in the country. The first noticeable effect of that national exposure on White's career was the auspicious reception given *The Real Issue* when it appeared in late November. For it was reviewed quickly, widely, and favorably, and within three months was in its fourth "edition." Almost immediately Samuel S. Mc-Clure arranged with White to reprint two of the stories in *McClure's Magazine* and contracted with him to write another half dozen for the magazine, then published them in book form in 1899 as *The Court of Boyville*.

Early in February 1897 Will traveled east of the Mississippi for the first time—to Chicago at the invitation of his publishers, where he met a number of regional writers and journalists, such as Hamlin Garland, Peter Finley Dunne, George Ade and Booth Tarkington—then on to Zanesville, Ohio, where Hanna had arranged that he be one of the speakers at the Lincoln Day banquet of the Ohio Republicans. Afterward Hanna insisted he go to Canton, Ohio, to meet President-elect McKinley, who had not attended the banquet on the excuse of illness. As a reporter for the *Star* White had spent a day with McKinley on a campaign swing through Kansas two years earlier and was then decidedly unimpressed, but dutifully he went to Canton with a letter from Hanna that ended, at Will's request, "He wants no office." As if unable to believe such a disclaimer, Mc-Kinley received him so coldly that when White got back to Emporia, he had the letter framed and hung on his office wall as a reminder to keep his resolution never to seek public office.

The letter notwithstanding, White was embarrassed early that summer by rumors he was to be named Emporia postmaster as the compromise candidate in a patronage battle between opposing factions of the state party. To prevent that, he and Sallie got railroad passes and set out for Washington on their first trip to the East Coast. There Hanna ushered him into the White House, where he again made his strange request to McKinley, who agreed this time to honor it. Several days later, while still in Washington, Will was introduced by Kansas Congressman Charles Curtis to Theodore Roosevelt (TR), then assistant secretary of the Navy. That introduction changed White's life: it provided him with a permanent political hero, who started his political transformation from conservative to liberal. They had lunch together the next day, and Roosevelt's talk chipped at White's previously unexamined faith in plutocracy and in its philosophical justification through Social Darwinism, the materialistic belief in "natural selection," which consequently called for a laissez-faire attitude toward society. From that day he slowly began to share Roosevelt's belief in moral idealism as motivation for human conduct, a belief outlined for him several months later when TR sent him his new book, *American Ideals and Other Essays.*

Before returning to Emporia White caught the train to New York City to spend a day with Sam McClure and his editorial staff. He found them compatible and exciting, somewhat like TR. As a group they were Middlewest and middle class in outlook and evinced a social idealism that formed the moral force behind the Muckraking Movement of the next decade. That McClure group was his New York coterie for the next fifteen years; he treasured their friendships for the rest of his life and profited by their widespread contacts. His first experience of those contacts was that very day when they set up an interview for him with his literary idol, the novelist William Dean Howells, who had read *The Real Issue* and praised it. Through them White gained an entrée to the Eastern magazine market. After returning home from that trip, he received a letter from Robert Bridges of *Scribner's Magazine* asking him to write several long fictionalized sketches based on Kansas politics; over the next four years White wrote five such stories for that magazine, which he then collected and published in book form as *Strategems and Spoils* (1901). Also in 1897 he wrote feature articles about his state's economy and culture for *Forum, Atlantic Monthly*, and *Scribner's*. Soon he had more requests for magazine pieces than he could handle, and became a regular contributor to *Collier's* and the *Saturday Evening Post*, in addition to *McClure's*. These three were among the five or six most popular and influential magazines of the Progressive Era and gave him a forum far beyond the bounds of Emporia and Kansas.

Yet in 1897 he was but a twenty-nine-year-old small-town newspaper editor who through the apt, hyperbolic humor of a widely reprinted editorial had contributed to McKinley's victorious campaign and by chance had capitalized on the publicity with the publication of a collection of newspaper short stories. His intellectual horizons were very much limited to provincial matters and conservative Republican attitudes. But that would change until eventually he had a national, even international vision and had marched in the vanguard of the Progressive party. Meanwhile, in the next several years he focused his energies on editing the *Gazette*, on helping direct local politics, and on developing a career as a writer of magazine short stories and features. In 1897 the *Gazette* was getting on its feet financially, partially because White had wrested city and county printing from Eskridge's *Republican* and had secured state Pension Office printing from Cy Leland, but also because income from his outside writing helped pay off the original debt of $3,000. That outside income then gave him the courage in 1899 to borrow for a new *Gazette* building and buy an impressive house on what was to become the less fashionable side of town.[13] Without that additional income he would have been but another small-town editor worried about meeting a payroll and interest on the mortgage.

When Will heard about the sinking of the U.S.S. *Maine* in February 1898, he realized dimly that that event signaled an end to an era, that America was no longer securely isolated, but that outside events from the gold strikes in Alaska and Australia to the Boer War in South Africa, would influence with increased significance domestic markets and politics. Though he resisted editorially the jingoistic fervor of the Spanish American War, developed and exploited by the yellow journalism of William R. Hearst and Joseph Pulitzer, it affected him personally just the same. For that war started his close college friend Fred Funston, who had been fighting with the Cuban revolutionaries, on his U.S. Army career and catapulted Teddy Roosevelt, the Cuban Rough Rider, into the governorship of New York. But at the time White was more concerned about things at home. Sallie was again not well the summer of 1898 and Will took her to Colorado, using his railroad pass to commute back and forth to Emporia. He was hard at work on his short stories for *McClure's* and on other magazine pieces and troubled by his knowledge of the impending criminal failure of a local banker and friend, Charlie C. Cross, who soon committed suicide.

White was also very busy in 1899. Governor Roosevelt came through Kansas in June en route to a meeting on the West Coast, and White rode with him through the state, handling introductions and publicity with his eye on a presidential boom in 1904. That spring the publishing firm of Way and Williams failed, and White had to go to Chicago in July to negotiate the purchase of *The Real Issue* by the firm of Doubleday & McClure. Then in imitation of Ed Howe at Atchinson he sponsored a successful late-summer street fair in Emporia with parades and booths, contests and tent shows, and Indians and the first automobile ever to appear west of Missouri, which he had arranged for on his trip to Chicago. That street fair made him locally. In the fall William Dean Howells stopped in Emporia to give a lecture at the Normal College, and the Whites, regarding him as the dean of American letters, held a dinner in his honor in their new home. Though nearly ruined by a panicky hired girl's taking French leave, that dinner party was to be the first of many for out-of-town notables. As White once summed up that evening, "since that day men who were to be president and men who had been president have sat around that oval table. Major generals, cabinet officers, powerful politicians, literary pundits and J. P. Morgan's family have poked their pink toes under it. But no one ever sat there of whom the host and hostess stood in such awe then and since, the greatest of them all."[14] The Whites were now somebodies in local society.

Another election year was 1900, and that meant White was busy with local politics in addition to overseeing completion of his new office building. He was also gradually rethinking his position toward government and social change, and in the process officially switching his internal party allegiance from Mark Hanna to Teddy Roosevelt. Indeed, two of White's most salient traits, both as a practical politician and as a social commentator, were his capacity for intellectual growth and his readiness to change positions; inexorably he kept just ahead of liberal Middlewestern middle-class public opinion for four decades, which was the source of his eventual reputation as a grass-roots sage. In the spring he went to Lincoln, Nebraska, to interview William Jennings Bryan for a character sketch commissioned by *McClure's Magazine*. It was the first of a number of interpretive, sometimes controversial magazine articles about politicians that he wrote over the next nearly three decades, then edited for his book *Masks in a Pageant* (1928). In June he planned to go to Philadelphia to cover the Republican national convention for *McClure's* news-paper syndicate but stayed home because Sallie was having a difficult time in the last month of pregnancy. On 17 June their first child to live, William Lindsay, was born.

At the convention New York Republican boss Senator Thomas Platt engineered Roosevelt's nomination to the vice-presidency to get the bothersome Teddy out of New York politics, and to spite Hanna. Though White had advised Roosevelt not to get shunted on to that side track, he supported the ticket enthusiastically because he was already boosting TR as a presidential candidate in 1904. Then just after the election he traveled to New York City to gather material for a *McClure's* sketch about Richard Croker, notorious Tammany boss. While there several publishers tempted him with editorial job offers, but he turned them down, as he did many subsequent offers over the years, in order to remain an independent editor and free-lance author at home in a small Kansas town. Yet at that time he did agree with George H. Lorimer, editor of the *Saturday Evening Post*, to write occasional interpretive articles, and his magazine contributions continued to increase.

Free-lance Publicist and Amateur Politician

During 1901 White continued to manage the *Gazette*, tend to political chores, and meet his magazine commitments, which included interviews that spring with former Presidents Benjamin Harrison and Grover Cleveland for later interpretive biographical sketches. In July, on behalf of the *Saturday Evening Post* he covered the opening of Indian lands around Lawton, Oklahoma, one of the last public land rushes in American history. Then in August he met with Vice-President Roosevelt at Colorado Springs to help set up a 1904 campaign for the presidency. The last week of August he went East, first to Canton, Ohio, to interview President McKinley for a *McClure's* article, then on to New York City to gather material and interview Senator Thomas C. Platt for another. From New York he planned to go to Washington to confer with Roosevelt about the "situation" and interview other politicians as background for his several projected sketches. But then McKinley was shot and after a week died. White found himself having dinner with Roosevelt his first night in Washington as president, with the "situation" drastically changed. Soon Will A. White was publicly tagged an intimate of the president and,

until the Rough Rider's own death in 1919, shared his political fortunes. That intimacy further stimulated his questioning of conservative socioeconomic assumptions and led to his following Roosevelt in
1912 to the Progressive party. His fellowship with the new president
in 1901 immediately increased his local political stature, because of
federal patronage, and enhanced his authority as a political publicist
and pundit. Thus that December when *McClure's Magazine* published
his hard-hitting, derogatory sketch of Platt as a political boss, the
senator assumed its animus inspired by Roosevelt and publicly threatened *McClure's* and White with a libel suit, which he never filed
despite much bluster.

For nearly seven years now White had worked hard as a newspaper
editor and magazine writer. In that time he had also published three
books and participated vigorously in local, state, and national politics.
Because of that frenetic pace, midway through January 1902 he experienced a nervous collapse. Following doctor's orders he took a
complete rest with Sallie on the then sparsely populated Catalina
Island just off the southern California coast, leaving their son with
Grandma White, and the *Gazette* to his staff. When he returned in
May, he had regained his health and returned to harness. But he
always worked at a gallop, and several times later in life suffered
similarly from nervous exhaustion and took extended rests.

Late in June Roosevelt invited him to Washington to consult
about patronage and the coming state elections. Later that year, prob-
ably at Roosevelt's suggestion, White wrote an article for the *Saturday
Evening Post* explaining the president's motives in launching a crusade against "bad trusts" with a suit against the Northern Securities
Company which stunned conservatives. In this article, not only did
White act effectively as Roosevelt's publicist, but he also revealed
his new attitude toward plutocracy, a change effected not only by
TR but also by the staff at *McClure's*. Three of his friends there—
Lincoln Steffens, Ida Tarbell, and Ray Stannard Baker—were to begin
somewhat self-consciously in the January 1903 issue a far-reaching
social crusade, later dubbed the Muckraking Movement, that was
fueled over the next decade by rapid-fire exposés in the major weekly
magazines. Though White wrote extensively during that era for
magazines identified with that movement and was in sympathy with
its aims, he was not a Muckraker per se, for he was far too impressionistic in method and ebullient in style and attitude. Though never
a clown, he provided readers of those magazines with welcome

humorous relief, especially when that crusade of exposure became too self-righteously sensational.

In September 1902 White traveled to southern Idaho to gather material for three articles for the *Saturday Evening Post* about gold strikes in the Thunder Mountain region. In Boise he renewed his friendship with the corporation lawyer William E. Borah, formerly a fellow student at the University of Kansas, who in 1906 was elected by the citizens of Idaho to the U.S. Senate, serving there until his death in 1940. Early in 1903 he helped White get out of a fraudulent federal land deal he innocently bought into with some Idaho railroad officials; White returned the favor when Borah was later falsely indicted by political enemies for timber fraud. In the *Autobiography*, White cited his involvement in that land deal as a personal lesson in how plutocracy skirts legality. Another relatively innocent brush with chicanery resulted from a second trip he made to the Idaho Thunder Mountain region, this time in the fall of 1903 and with Lewis C. Van Riper, shady gold mine developer and editor of the *United States Mining Journal*, a monthly published in New York City to promote gold mine investments. In return for 10,000 pooled shares of mining stock, White wrote a long article about the region for that journal, which without his consent was broken into two parts and rewritten to laud the mining possibilities of the area and puff unsound mining firms.[15] Later, political foes questioned his ethics in this connection to his great embarrassment and lame protests. Thus he learned painfully how "malefactors of great wealth" worked, firsthand lessons that also helped propel him into the vanguard of the Progressives.

In February 1903 White went to Washington to gather data and impressions for another series of articles in the *Saturday Evening Post* analyzing and praising Roosevelt's administration and his drive against the monopolies. During the first part of that year White also pushed for an investigation of frauds in the Post Office Department's Rural Free Delivery system that involved a number of Republican congressmen. He helped Joseph L. Bristow, an old Kansas friend and at that time an assistant postmaster general whom Roosevelt had selected as a special investigator, to gather the data that put in prison U.S. Senator Joseph R. Burton of Kansas, a political enemy of White's, and led to seventy-four other indictments.

After recovering from a tough bout with pneumonia that winter, White jumped headlong into the politics of 1904 with magazine ar-

ticles and newspaper editorials that captured national attention. Ex-
uberantly, he eulogized Roosevelt and pushed for his nomination,
covered both the Republican and Democratic conventions in June,
and returned home just in time for the birth of his daughter, Mary.
She was a sickly baby, so later that summer Sallie took her to the
Colorado mountains to escape the Kansas heat; after that, summers
in Colorado became an annual ritual for the Whites, leading to their
buying a cabin within sight of Long's Peak near Estes Park. But that
year state politics kept Will in Emporia. He had joined a group of
insurgent Republicans who backed the gubernatorial candidacy of
Edward W. Hoch to fight the state Republican machine led by Cy
Leland. And for the first time White broke party regularity by endorsing Joseph W. Folk, Democratic candidate for governor of Missouri, in a strong editorial stance in which he underscored the need
for honesty in government. From then on White was enough of a
maverick in his editorials to establish credibility among independents
and dismay among GOP regulars, though to his wing of the Kansas
party his allegiance was thorough and unbroken even during Bull
Moose days. After his candidates won in November, White wrote a
roseate assessment for the *Saturday Evening Post* of the liberal implications of the election that greatly pleased Roosevelt and demonstrated
White's total commitment to the "Square Deal." Indeed, within the
next decade he became in some ways more genuinely liberal than his
mentor.

Because he knew railroads were the major powers controlling the
Kansas Republican machine, White put his editorial weight during
the spring of 1905 behind a bill pending in the state legislature
against issuing railroad passes to politicians. He suggested including
journalists too, though he himself held several passes in return for
free advertising. That bill remained an important state issue for several years, and the next year White followed up on his convictions
by no longer accepting railroad passes. He had also on principle refused to sign advertising contracts for patent medicines, because they
allowed the companies to cancel if material in any way injurious to
them appeared in his paper, which, of course, blocked publicity or
comment about their practices. White furnished Mark Sullivan, who
was investigating patent medicine frauds for *Collier's*, information
about those practices and copies of the contracts, which he reprinted
in his exposé. But the extent to which White by 1905 had broken
with the Social Darwinism of "What's the Matter with Kansas?" is

best shown by his warm support of Governor Hoch's proposal for a state-owned oil refinery to counter Standard Oil's monopoly. When Ida Tarbell, who over the previous two years had published her famous muckraking history of Standard Oil in *McClure's*, came to Kansas to investigate Hoch's proposal, White helped her meet the right people and gather data.

In March 1905 he proudly accepted the only state office he would ever hold. Hoch appointed him a member of the Board of Regents of the University of Kansas. Over the next seven years under governors Hoch and Walter R. Stubbs, both liberal Republicans, he worked hard with Chancellor Frank H. Strong to build the university in a period of rapid change and growth, resigning only after his faction lost the state house and he believed himself a political liability to the school. And during 1905–6, in addition to writing more than a dozen articles for various magazines, White wrote a series of eighteen short fictional sketches for the *Saturday Evening Post* about life as seen from the office of a small county-seat newspaper, which were published in book form as *In Our Town* (1906). They reflected a humorous, sentimental side of small-town life and pleased many, with Mark Twain, for example, writing White, "Howells told me that 'In Our Town' was a charming book, and indeed it is."[16] Though busy with his many writing commitments and his young family, he continued in the early part of 1906 his state fight against railroads in politics, and pushed also for a direct primary system of nominating candidates and direct election of U.S. senators. His liberal faction of the party secured the governorship, but it was outmaneuvered in the legislature by the Old Guard who elected to the U.S. senate the railroads' candidate, Charles Curtis, a sometime friend of Will's but at this time an interparty foe.

Early that fall, instead of following the state campaigns, he spent much of his time back East helping organize a new muckraking magazine. John S. Phillips, long-time associate editor of *McClure's*, had quit in a dispute with Sam McClure and was joined by Ida Tarbell, Lincoln Steffens, and Ray Stannard Baker, plus others, in buying the venerable *Leslie's Monthly*, which they hoped would become the new standard-bearer of reform. With that in mind they renamed it the *American Magazine* and asked Finley Peter Dunne and White to join them as associate editors to leaven their seriousness with good humor and whimsical points of view. For the first issue of the new magazine White wrote an article entitled "The Partnership of Society" which proclaimed the moral spirit behind the reform movement so well that it moved Roosevelt to declare, "I feel as I ought to have written it myself."[17] But White's association with that magazine, though heartfelt, was in fact limited because of his continuing commitments to other magazines, to politics and the *Gazette*, and to the writing of a novel. Off and on during 1906 he worked on *A Certain Rich Man*, a novel that traces the career of John Barclay, a ruthless Kansas businessman and eventual trust magnate. The plot supports a heavily didactic theme: at the end of his life John finally sees the spiritual emptiness of his all-consuming pursuit of wealth, rejects it, and adopts altruism.

Through the spring of 1907 White turned his attention to helping organize the state's liberal Republicans for 1908, then took the family to Colorado for the summer, where he devoted himself to his novel. But the book took more than another year to finish because of the demands of the 1908 campaign. Kansas had just adopted primary laws and two of White's closest political allies, Walter R. Stubbs and Joseph Bristow, were running for governor and U.S. senator in the primaries. But Bristow's campaign against incumbent conservative Senator Chester Long ran into trouble and White sweated through a hot summer electioneering. He persuaded Norman Hapgood to commission an article for *Collier's* against Long's conservative record, he compiled an exposé of Long's voting record which he placed in the *Kansas City Star* and elsewhere, and he even rented a circus tent for rallies that he organized throughout eastern Kansas featuring Wisconsin Senator Bob La Follette, foremost congressional Republican liberal.[18] White also covered the national conventions for the Adams news syndicate and wrote several magazine articles at Roosevelt's suggestion supporting William Howard Taft's candidacy, though from the first he was not as enthusiastic about Taft as TR. In August both Stubbs and Bristow won the Republican primaries, which in Kansas in that era was tantamount to election, and White could shift from publicist to author. That fall and winter he finished revising his novel and wrote for the *American Magazine* most of a serious series of lead articles that appeared through 1909. In them he analyzed and forecast changes in American democracy from an idealistic perspective of social altruism; the Macmillan firm published them in book form the next year as *The Old Order Changeth*. It became a standard handbook to contemporary political and social reform.

In 1907 White had hired an alcoholic tramp journalist named Walt Mason and helped him kick the habit. He was a facile writer and by chance began to turn out daily prose verses for the *Gazette* under the head "Uncle Walt Says" which were immediately popular and often copied on exchange by other newspapers. They caught the attention of George M. Adams, who arranged their syndication through White; eventually they were carried by more than 200 newspapers and made Mason passing famous. With Mason to handle the editorial page, and two dependable long-time staff members to boss the *Gazette*, Laura French the managing editor and Walter Hughes the business manager, White felt free in March 1909 to take his family and mother to Europe for a six-month tour. It was their first time abroad. Landing first at Naples, they did the grand tour, plus England and Ireland, a tour important to editor White, so he reports in the *Autobiography*, because "it was a milepost. In the new environment of Europe, I saw myself in perspective" (408). On shipboard on their way back he and Sallie discovered through a half-page advertisement in the *New York Times* that *A Certain Rich Man* had been out but three weeks and was already "in its fourth large printing." Thus White returned to Emporia at the end of August a bestselling novelist. To his embarrassment the townspeople and other Kansas friends greeted him with a band, songs, and an elaborate program of skits based on the novel.

While White was in Europe, Roosevelt was off for a year of big-game hunting in Africa, ostensibly to give Taft a free hand with the presidency. As one of his first acts, Taft issued a call much desired by Republican liberals for a special session of Congress to revise the old Dingley Tariff downward, yet he ended up supporting the new, higher Payne-Aldrich Tariff and thus appeared to align himself with the conservative wing of the party. Appearance became reality during the winter of 1909–10 after the liberal wing's successful attempt to spike Speaker of the House "Uncle Joe" Cannon and after the hullabaloo surrounding the Pinchot-Ballinger affair. Cannon was so powerful under the procedures of the House that he had blocked much reform legislation since becoming speaker in 1905; even TR had hung back from challenging him. But Taft, irked by Cannon's crudity, at first encouraged the movement to limit his power, then in the heat of battle apparently changed his mind. After the insurgents won and changed the makeup of the House Committee on Rules, they viewed Taft's involvement as devious and immediately pushed through Congress the Mann-Elkins Act of 1910 further regulating railroads, which went well beyond Taft's wishes. By then Gifford Pinchot, who had been appointed chief forester by Roosevelt, had accused his boss, Secretary of the Interior Richard A. Ballinger, of fraud in leasing federal lands to certain large corporations. Taft upheld his secretary and reluctantly dismissed Pinchot amid considerable public clamor.

From these events came the term "Progressive," or the at first more popular "Insurgent," to identify those congressional liberal Republicans who had marshaled behind TR's moderate drive for reform from 1903 on and late in 1909 came to believe that drive abandoned by Taft. Today American historians call political liberals of both parties in the first two decades of this century "progressives," and loosely designate that period of reform activity the "Progressive Movement." But early in 1910 Progressive Republican congressman lacked such historical perspective and saw themselves an endangered species. Soon Roosevelt returned from Africa and allowed himself to get caught up in the Progressives' anger at the president, who was using his office to build conservative strength in the Midwest in anticipation of the congressional elections of 1910. The Progressives were strongest in the Midwest and felt betrayed by TR's hand-picked successor. In addition, Roosevelt believed himself personally slighted by Taft, and their friendship cooled rapidly and publicly. By now the Republican party was badly fragmented.[19]

Will, of course, after his return from Europe joined the interparty battle, but in his own way. Though morally earnest in his commitments, he was seldom solemn about political matters. And in this era of reform he was having the time of his life. In fact, a spirit of exhilaration typified the Progressive Movement, a spirit he captured in burlesque doggerel in a *Gazette* editorial of 10 December 1909 headed "Insurgents":

O come, my love, insurge with me, adown the bosky dell; we'll chase the nimble octopus across the barren fell; the moon is high, the tariff, too, is rising every hour; so come, my love, insurge with me, here in my sylvan bower. Yes, come, my love, and trip with me the light fantastic toe; and as we slip along let's trip our agile Uncle Joe. The differentials are in bloom, the ad valorem beams; the rules are moaning at the bar, while dimpled freedom screams. Then come, my love, let us insurge; Ah, let us rage and snort; O let us paw the soft lush grass, while our two souls cavort. The time is ripe, the hour is here, our song will be no dirge; O let us whoop and fly the coop—come on, O let's insurge.

When White learned that TR was on his way out of Africa, he wrote to him at length analyzing the "situation." But he believed strongly that no man should seek a third presidential term, so for some time he leaned toward Senator Bob La Follette as the proper Progressive to challenge Taft. But Will's heart was with TR, especially after his swing through the Midwest in August in support of beleaguered Insurgents. During that tour Roosevelt gave the most famous speech of his career, at Osawatomie, Kansas, in which he announced a "New Nationalism" that advocated a welfare state along the lines that Herbert Croly, a New York editor and social critic, had enumerated a year earlier in his provocative book *The Promise of American Life.* In that speech, ghostwritten by Gifford Pinchot with some help from White, Roosevelt championed a number of specific legislative reforms that would advance popular government. Yet the philosophical thrust of New Nationalism itself was anti-Jeffersonian, in that it abandoned trust-busting in favor of greatly enhanced governmental power to regulate both Big Business and labor, the ultimate implications of which were overlooked at first by Roosevelt's enthusiastic followers.[20] And one of those was White himself, who in that election year warmly welcomed TR's support on behalf of the Kansas Progressive Republicans. By this time he was a boss in Kansas politics and in fact had written much of the state platform that year. In November, in the face of national Democratic success, the Progressive Republicans carried Kansas.

Local politics did not take all his time, of course, for both the *Gazette* and his children were growing and claiming some of his attention. And he went Back East for several "personal" occasions: in February to confer with his friends at the *American Magazine* and give a speech at Columbia University, then again in May to receive an honorary degree from Columbia and deliver an address entitled "A Theory of Spiritual Progress" before its Phi Beta Kappa Society (published in pamphlet form by "The Gazette Press"). But he was deeply committed to politics and through 1911 and 1912 canvassed his state and the Midwest in support of Progressive Republicans. Also, he wrote nearly a dozen magazine articles explaining the Progressive position. During the summer of 1911, though, he retired with his family to the Colorado mountains, where in peace he started a second novel, *In the Heart of a Fool* (1918), a long fictional treatment of contemporary social problems. But politics interrupted his work on it so often in the next few years that by the time he finished it, the national mood had changed and the book never caught on.

Progressive Republican

On 2 February 1912 Senator La Follette suffered a temporary but embarrassing nervous collapse during a speech before a publisher's convention in Philadelphia. That gave many of his supporters, including White, the excuse they needed to jump to Roosevelt as the strong man to oppose Taft for the 1912 Republican presidential nomination. Once committed White never let grass grow over his toes. In early February he was in Washington conferring with prominent Congressional progressives about Roosevelt's campaign. They had only four months to organize against Taft's conservative machine and against La Follette, who remained in the fight. When the convention met in Chicago in mid-June, White was there wearing two hats; he was a Republican National committeeman from Kansas and a reporter for the Adams newspaper syndicate. He was also one of TR's convention strategists. But emotions, not strategy, ruled. After the Taft group captured the credentials committee and a compromise on White's old friend Missouri Governor Herbert Hadley as presidential candidate failed, Roosevelt personally led his forces out of the party. White then covered the Democratic convention in Baltimore, where after a bitter battle the progressive Woodrow Wilson was nominated on the forty-sixth ballot.

The first week of August White was back in Chicago to help organize the Progressive or Bull Moose party. In its ostensible devotion to reform it was a resurrection of the People's party of the 1890s. And he freely acknowledged the irony of the author of the most famous diatribe against the Populists—"What's the Matter with Kansas?"—becoming a leader in this party. But he now believed wholeheartedly in the need for reform and believed that this new party, in contrast to the old ragtag People's party, represented respectable middle-class opinion led by socially responsible men. In addition, he was mesmerized by TR, overlooked his egocentric drive for power, and did not note at first what he regarded later as the cynical motives of several key delegates, especially two of Roosevelt's closest advisers, the millionaire banker George W. Perkins and publisher Frank A. Munsey. White was also boxed in personally: as an idealistic progressive he felt unable to support the old Republican machine, yet as a practical politician he knew Kansas as a one-party state where to be a Democrat was certifiably quixotic. And, too, all his life he believed the Democratic party—led even by Wilson or FDR—to be an immoral partnership of the conservative South with the corrupt big city machines of the North. So with many of his Kansas political friends he bolted to the Bull Moosers. But because of the confusion caused by that bolt Progressives at the state level ran on the Republican slate in Kansas and out of pique, party regulars voted for Democrats. Thus that bolt threw the Kansas election to Wilson and to a Democratic governor and U.S. senator. Because many of the Kansas Progressive Republicans had left the national organization, they lost their hard-won position in the state party and at the same time, because of defeat at the polls, lost their power base in public office.

In the next four years, with Wilson following a liberal program, the Progressive party lost much of its incipient theoretical appeal and practical support. Yet White committed himself to that party until its inglorious end in 1916. For the first five months of 1913 the Whites rested in La Jolla, California, with Will working on his novel. After he made a speaking tour in May to help Governor Hiram Johnson and his California Progressive party, they returned briefly to Emporia, then went to Colorado for the summer, where he continued with the novel. But after returning to his desk at the *Gazette* in the fall of 1913, he was again fully embroiled in politics, stirring the wrath of standpat Republicans by praising editorially the progressive reforms of Democrat President Wilson and Kansas Governor George H. Hodges, and by writing many letters and speaking across the state for the Bull Moosers. Through 1914, in fact, he gave most of his attention to building that party and consequently was stunned by its dismal showing in the fall returns. He did not lose faith, though, but planned for 1916 and resisted at first any talk of fusion with the Republicans. For he did not anticipate the oversized, bruised ego of TR, who refused a martyr's role as minority third-party candidate again, or the stubborn cleverness of George Perkins, who led the Progressives to try to secure the Republican nomination for Roosevelt, or the diplomatic crises of a world war which diverted national attention from domestic issues.

In Colorado during the summer of 1915 White worked doggedly at his second novel and also wrote several short stories with social problem themes which appeared in *Collier's* or the *Saturday Evening Post* then were collected as the book, *God's Puppets* (1916). That fall he and Sallie spent two months in the East, as they were to do more frequently from then on, to visit friends, attend concerts, plays, and public dinners, and confer with politicians, publishers, and magazine editors. By mid-January 1916, when White attended a strategy meeting of the Progressive National Committee in Chicago, he had come to realize the most practical course to follow was fusion with the Republicans, hopefully behind Roosevelt. But that seemed possible to him only if the Republicans faced the threat of a Progressive party truly ready to go to the polls.

In June he returned to Chicago as a national committeeman to the Progressive party convention and to cover it and the simultaneous Republican convention for the Adams syndicate. The strategy of most Progressives was to nominate Roosevelt immediately, hoping that would move the Republicans to nominate him also, rather than face another divisive national election. If that joint nomination were impossible, then they could arrange for a compromise candidate and platform. However, Perkins, whom White thoroughly distrusted, in consultation with TR prevented an early nomination because they thought it would stop any chance of a nod from the Republicans. Despite several conferences, the managers of neither party could settle on a compromise candidate. After Charles Evans Hughes was selected by the Republicans, Roosevelt callously rejected a late-hour Progressive nomination and the party died in agony, with most of the delegates feeling used and betrayed, some even more so when TR managed to get the Progressive National Committee to endorse Hughes two weeks later. In his autobiography White remembered that as "the end of a great adventure, politically and emotionally probably the greatest adventure of my life" (527).

Chapter Two

The Progressive as Dissenter: 1916-1944

Reporter of War and Peace

The European war sapped American politics in 1916. In June Will White had written Rodney A. Elward, a Kansas "La Follettite" Republican, "the whole trouble with our humanitarian platform, as I see it at the moment, is that it hit war.... You cannot get humanitarian progress on the front page when humanitarian retrogression is occupying the headlines."[1] During the campaign that fall Republican presidential nominee Charles Evans Hughes equivocated so on the issue of war and peace that Democrats tagged him Charles "Evasive" Hughes. In spite of that, Theodore Roosevelt stumped hard for him, hoping thereby to mend the party split, but enough Progressives sat the election out or voted for Woodrow Wilson to bring about his reelection. White was among the sitters, though he did support Hughes nominally in order to regain a place in Kansas politics. By January 1917 he was editorially defending Wilson's cautious preparation for war, to the disgust of TR the firebrand. After Congress declared war in April against the Central Powers, White patriotically supported Wilson's leadership.

In August, four months after the United States had entered the war, Will and his old friend Henry J. Allen, publisher of the *Wichita Eagle*, sailed to France as official Red Cross observers to inspect the work of that agency. They spent two months in Europe, sometimes at the battle fronts, then returned to Kansas to publicize Red Cross activities. Allen soon returned to France to work as a volunteer for that agency, but White remained at home to write a series of syndicated newspaper articles praising its work and to speak on its behalf throughout the Midwest. That winter he finished his much-interrupted novel, *In the Heart of a Fool*, and sent it off to the publisher. He also rewrote the letters that he had sent Sallie from Europe to fit them

into a slight, fictional plot, added material from some of his syndicated articles, and published them as *The Martial Adventures of
Henry and Me* (1918), a book that caught the public mood and
proved popular. Curiously, this tale was part of White's strategy to
return to political power in Kansas, because early in the congressional
election year of 1918 he began a campaign for Henry Allen as
liberal Republican candidate for governor, while Allen remained in
France working for the Red Cross. His letters to Will Hays, chairman of the Republican National Committee, urged him fervently to
work to keep the party from turning so reactionary that it drove
away shipwrecked Progressives. Allen won the primary and governorship, and White was again a force in the state party, but not in the
national organization, as he found out in the next several years.

In December 1918 White went to France with his son Bill to
cover the Peace Conference for the Wheeler syndicate and observe
for the Red Cross. In New York before boarding ship he visited TR,
who was ill and hospitalized, and they talked somewhat wistfully of
presidential possibilities for 1920, but Roosevelt died the next month
and White lost his greatest political hero. Wilson and the Peace Conference had riveted public attention on Paris; there White was sur-
rounded by friends and acquaintances, a miniature who's who of
American journalism. Ray Stannard Baker was in charge of press relations for the American Peace Commission, and most of the old
McClure's staff were covering the conference. Because of his wide
variety of contacts and the respect he commanded among journalists,
White became an unofficial spokesman for the American press group
as they protested their exclusion from meetings of the Allies. His
stature as an independent editor was so well known that Wilson
appointed him, and diplomat George D. Herron, to represent the
United States at a proposed meeting with representatives of Soviet
Russia, France, Britain, and various small Baltic states at Prinkipo, a
Turkish island near the Dardanelles. The Allies had not established
diplomatic relations with the new Soviet government, which was not
represented at the Peace Conference, and this meeting was to prepare
for that. White was sympathetic with the Russian revolution and
interested in some of the Bolshevik aims. But after much preliminary
negotiation, the French, who were following their own version of
European political power, blocked that proposal and conference;
those negotiations, however, gave White a clearer insight into European politics and a lasting skepticism of French political aims.

When he returned home in June 1919, he knew at first hand the Parisian quagmire Wilson had slogged through in pursuit of his Fourteen Points; he admired the courage of the man and thought him successful, by and large. He also perceived weaknesses in the peace treaty and because of them believed the United States must enter the League of Nations to insure world peace. He could not anticipate, of course, Wilson's stroke and personal stubbornness, nor the political vindictiveness of Republican Senator Henry Cabot Lodge and others. From Emporia White fought for the League, writing letters, editorials, and magazine articles, and giving speeches under the auspices of the League to Enforce Peace. But Wilson would accept no reservations to his treaty, and the Senate rejected the League, even though a solid majority of the senators and most of the American people favored some version of it. Knowing the fragility of the European settlement, White saw the tragedy of that rejection.

He was also deeply disturbed by changes in the national mood. Only a week after the declaration of war Wilson had appointed the former muckraker George Creel to lead a propaganda bureau, the Committee on Public Information. Creel used the revolution in mass communications, hitherto virtually untapped, and its brilliant personnel to rally public support behind the war effort. The public responded with naive fervor. In an excess of wartime renunciation the country even passed the Eighteenth Amendment and the Volstead Act prohibiting the manufacture and sale of alcoholic beverages, moves that greatly pleased White who, as he grew older, became an intemperate prohibitionist. But persistent advocacy of altruism during the progressive years, then strident calls "to save the world for democracy" during and just after the war, had taken their toll; much of the public were tired of appeals to higher morality. Instead they were moved to unthinking hysteria as Attorney General A. Wilson Palmer launched his infamous "Red hunt" on New Year's Day 1920, encouraging reactionaries in the guise of superpatriots to attack as un-American liberals and liberal ideas everywhere. So Will A. White, moderate liberal and as American as warm apple pie, spent much of the following decade fighting the spell of rampant reaction.

Troubled Critic of "Normalcy"

In June 1920 White again attended a Republican national convention in Chicago as a delegate and syndicated reporter. Though he

served on the platform committee, he watched helpless as the leading Senate reactionaries turned the party over to Senator Warren G.
Harding, his Ohio gang, and his pledge to return the country to
"normalcy." White then covered the Democratic convention in San
Francisco, where the Democrats nominated progressive Ohio Governor James Cox on a strong reform platform that unequivocally en-
dorsed the peace treaty and the League. If it were a matter of logic,
White should have supported Cox, but logic did not control Kansas
politics nor his loyalties and prejudices, so he ignored his national
constituency, swallowed hard, and took the Republican bit. But that
did not mean he liked its taste. In a letter of 8 September 1920 to
Charles F. Scott, a fellow Kansas newspaper editor, he wrote "I am
low in my mind politically, but am coming through supporting the
Republican ticket with about as much enthusiasm as a man has when
he puts on his evening suit and goes out to usher at his best girl's
wedding. I'm going to behave properly . . . and have my everlasting
regrets just the same."[2] After the elections he wrote Ray Stannard
Baker, "What a God-damned world this is! I trust you will realize
that I am not swearing; merely trying to express in the mildest terms
what I think of the conditions that exist. What a God-damned
world!"[3]

During 1920 and early 1921 White worked on a book about his
associations with Teddy Roosevelt, tentatively entitled "A Friend's
Chronicle" and in Colorado that summer started a series of magazine
short stories which he planned to gather in a book. But a sad event
put an end to both projects. In the spring of 1921 he had gone East
to make a speech before a bookseller's convention in Atlantic City
and to collect material for several articles about the Harding administration. While there he received a telegram from Sallie that their
daughter had taken a tumble from her horse, that she seemed unhurt
but in shock. Her condition worsened and he and his son Bill, who
was then attending Harvard, hurriedly caught trains back home.
At Chicago Will's close friends Edna Ferber and Harold Ickes met
his train to tell him Mary had died. The day after the funeral Will
sat down at his desk and, with Sallie at his side, wrote Mary's obituary.
It was such a touching editorial tribute to their daughter that it lives
still as his most widely known piece of writing. After the pain of her
death he could never go back to his book about TR or finish his
series of short stories, because he associated them too closely with her.
In fact, he never composed fiction again.

Yet he used writing as an anodyne. Three weeks after his daughter's death he wrote George H. Lorimer, editor of the *Saturday Evening Post*, "You would be doing me an infinite kindness if you could assign me some other subject than fiction from which I might make a running start back into writing. . . . I'm deaf and dumb and blind and my starter won't work. If you could give me a push with an order for anything on God's earth it would be a merciful kindness."[4] In the fall of 1921 he agreed to handle the editorial page for *Judge*, a well-known comic magazine. He churned out weekly "humorous" editorials for nearly a year but resigned after differing with the managing editor about their policy toward prohibition. Several months before that resignation he agreed to do a weekly feature for the *New York Sunday Tribune* headed "As I See It," starting July 1922, which he continued almost a year until it palled.[5] Never again would he do a regular feature. Various syndicates made him offers—even to replace Will Rogers when he was killed in a plane crash—but White refused to be tied once more to a column, explaining later to Frank Knox, publisher of the *Chicago Daily News*, "Whatever I do worth a tinker's damn is spontaneous. The minute I sign a contract I lose my spontaneity, which is the chief wellspring of my writing."[6]

That spontaneity earned him a Pulitzer prize for a 1922 *Gazette* editorial. In 1920 Kansas passed a law to put labor disputes in the hands of an industrial court which could compel arbitration. In July 1922 the railroad shopworkers, dissatisfied with their company unions after the U.S. Railroad Labor Board cut wages, called a national strike for the right to join with the Railroad Brotherhoods and retrieve some of that cut. Emporia was an important division point on the Santa Fe at that time, having a large railroad roundhouse with its accompanying shops. So White knew personally that these railroaders had a legitimate grievance. He had supported the Industrial Court Act as a way to bring about industrial peace, but when Governor Henry Allen prohibited picketing under that act, White criticized him. He pointed out that such a prohibition would eventually be ruled invalid in a strike involving federal issues and that the temporary effect would only be to support management and interfere with the rights of labor. Forbidden to strike, the shopworkers asked friendly merchants to display printed posters supporting the walkout. When Allen ordered all posters removed because he thought them a form of picketing, White denounced that action as an infringement of free speech, displayed a poster in the *Gazette* windows, and defied the governor to arrest him. Reluctantly, Allen asked the Kansas attorney general to issue an arrest warrant. After it was served, White removed his poster and prepared to defend his case in the courts. That arrest garnered much publicity, both because he and Allen were close friends and political cronies and because it raised fundamental First Amendment issues. Local public reaction was intense, with many conservative Kansas papers attacking White. During that outcry he replied to a friendly protest letter from a former fellow Bull Mooser; then, thinking that letter a strong defense in general, he edited his carbon copy and ran it in the *Gazette* as a front-page editorial headed "To An Anxious Friend." It is a brief but clearly reasoned, even passionate argument for freedom of speech during times of political stress. In it he put the essence of his life's moral philosophy, a tenacious belief in man's innate goodness, and declared his fundamental faith in social righteousness, during an era of moral fatigue.

Though White did vote for Harding in 1920, his public comments exhibit a painfully ambivalent attitude toward that presidency, alternately criticizing and praising the man and his cabinet. Perhaps he hoped to establish some personal influence with him, as he had with McKinley, Roosevelt, and even Wilson. He corresponded with Harding, sent him some of his published comments, and met with him both privately and together with others, but his hopes for influence waned as the scandals of that administration surfaced months before Harding's death in 1923. Looking back several years later on the politics of that time White wrote Brand Whitlock, widely known journalist and reformer, "The story of Babylon is a Sunday School story compared with the story of Washington from June 1919 until July 1923, and so far as that goes, considerably later. We haven't even yet got back to our Father's house. He can't see us even from afar off. It's invisible. And the whole thing is epitomized by the rise of Harding. If ever there was a man who was a he-harlot, it was this same Warren G. Harding."[7]

In 1924 White tried his best to turn Kansas "back to our Father's house." He ran for governor as an independent on essentially a single-issue anti–Ku Klux Klan platform. In the *Gazette* he had attacked the Klan from its start in Kansas early in 1921, but to little purpose because small-town and rural America responded readily to the Klan's simplistic morality and its easily identifiable scapegoats—Roman Catholics, Jews, and Negroes. By 1924 it had become such a strong force in the state that neither the Democrat nor the Republican candidate for governor would denounce the Klan, though the Democrats did have an anti–Klan statement in their platform. Furthermore, White suspected the Republican nominee, Ben Paulen, to be an active Klan sympathizer. In September he announced his independent candidacy, to the consternation of both parties, and began a vigorous six-week campaign tour around the state, chauffeured by his son Bill in the family Dodge and accompanied by Sallie, his "campaign manager." With his command of rhetoric and his eye for self-dramatization, White aimed at a national constituency, because he was running more against the Klan than for governor of Kansas. In his *Gazette* announcement of his candidacy, he concentrated on the larger issue of freedom and was somewhat restrained. But in his speeches during the campaign, in order to make good copy for the AP wire, he unleashed his faculty of ridicule at the claptrap of the Klan's fraternal structure and its naive bigotry; for instance: "The independent ticket for Governor and Lieutenant Governor is filed to protest against gag rule. The gag rule first came into the Republican Party last May when a flock of dragons, kleagles, cyclopses and fieries came up to Wichita from Oklahoma and held a meeting with some Kansas terrors, genii and whangdoodles. . . . A few weeks later the cyclopses, pterodactyls, kleagles, wizards and willopus-wallopuses began parading in the Kansas cow pastures, passing the word down to the shirt-tail rangers that they were to go into the Kansas primaries and nominate Ben Paulen."[8] White lost the election, coming in a close third, a few thousand votes behind the Democrat, but he did give support state-wide to anti–Klan Republicans and sharpened national focus on that era's most obvious instrument of reaction. While he deepened the machine politician's distrust of him as an uncontrollable maverick, he did enhance his national reputation as an independent political voice for freedom.[9]

In addition to his feature writing and his involvement in state politics, White wrote several books during the first half of the 1920s. Since 1919, when first approached by the Houghton Mifflin Company to contribute to its Modern American Statesman Series, he had thought of writing an extended biographical sketch of Woodrow Wilson, whose personality both fascinated and repelled him. During the latter part of 1923 he worked on that biography, traveling widely early in 1924 to interview those closest to the former president. Wilson died in February 1924 and White pushed to complete his sketch, publishing it late that year with the Houghton Mifflin Company as *Woodrow Wilson, the Man, His Times and His Task*. But in June he stopped work on that biography long enough to report the national conventions for the Bell syndicate and to write an article about them for *Collier's*. He then collected that material, edited and revised it, and published it with Macmillan's in book form as *Politics: The Citizen's Business*. It was issued in September as topical commentary and included reprints of key convention speeches and the platforms of both parties.

In 1920 when Calvin Coolidge first appeared in the national political scene, White was unimpressed, turning down a strongly urged request by Will Hayes, as a sop to the Progressives, to chair the pro forma committee to notify Coolidge of his vice-presidential nomination. But White changed his mind about the man as he watched that Vermont Yankee complete Harding's term untouched by the widening scandal of that administration. Regarding him as a sincere New England conservative, he supported him editorially in 1924 and soon after the election accepted a commission from *Collier's* to write a sketch of him. That sketch turned into a series of four articles plus two others that appeared in *Collier's* in the spring of 1925, which he quickly edited and issued as the book *Calvin Coolidge: The Man Who Is President* (1925). To the surprise of many liberals, White found this dour Yankee provincial, this honest servant of Big Business, genuinely interesting because he saw in him the moral spirit of the era. Late in 1925, in reply to a letter criticizing his favorable focus upon Coolidge, he wrote that the president "represents exactly the mood of the people. In a different mood he would not represent them of course. In the Roosevelt days he would have been impossible and out of line. But he is an honest, courageous, cautious, kindly conservative, and that is what the people want...."[10] In a further attempt to capture and explain that mood White wrote during the 1930s another more carefully researched biography of the man entitled *A Puritan in Babylon, the Story of Calvin Coolidge* (1938).

One measure of White's stature as a social commentator during the 1920s was an invitation in April 1925 to deliver the Weil Lectures on American Citizenship at the University of North Carolina. The university then published his group of five lectures as *Some Cycles of Cathay* (1925). Another was an invitation from its founder Harry Scherman to be one of the five original judges for the Book-of-the-Month Club. That organization was the first significant American book club; it set a pattern of quality for later clubs and became an important influence in shaping the reading habits of many Americans.

White was an intimate part of that influence: from 1926 to his death in 1944 he devoted many hours to helping select the monthly offerings.

Early in 1928 White attracted attention by twitting the Daughters of the American Revolution for distributing a pamphlet attacking many prominent liberals as subversives, including himself. He wrote several widely copied editorials satirizing the D.A.R. and then, after its officials replied in kind, accused that organization in an AP release of being the woman's auxiliary to the Ku Klux Klan: "The D.A.R. has yanked the Klan out of its cow pastures and set it down in the breakfast room of respectability, removing its hood and putting on a transformation, bobbing its shirt-tail uniform to knee lengths," parading "as the goddess of liberty" but allowing "several lengths of Ku Klux nighty to show under her red, white and blue."[11] He had fun with that tempest among the teacups, but regretted that his book *Masks in a Pageant* (1928) came out too late to capitalize on the publicity. In that book he assembled from his many magazine features of the previous thirty years interpretive sketches of fourteen representative politicians. It was his last collection of magazine materials, though others compiled selections from his editorials and letters. He was now sixty years old and wealthy by small-town standards. While age did not greatly diminish his vigor, it did his free-lance output: in the next decade he wrote only an occasional feature for the national magazine market, though he continued to contribute many short commentaries.

Age certainly did not diminish his appetite for politics. He was closely involved in the presidential campaign of 1928, having been an admirer of Herbert Hoover since meeting him and observing his relief work during the World War. From Vernon Kellogg, who was a close associate of Hoover's, White learned much more about the man and, persuaded somehow that he was a moderate liberal, suggested him editorially as a presidential candidate in both 1920 and 1924. For 1928 he did more than suggest; he invited him to Emporia in 1927 to meet a large gathering of Kansas newspaper editors and boomed his candidacy in speeches and editorials and in an ostensibly interpretive article for *Collier's*.[12] In June 1928 he was again both a syndicated reporter and delegate to the Republican convention, but because of state politics was pledged to a favorite son, Senator Charles Curtis, who did become the vice-presidential candidate. When Hoover gained the presidential nomination on the first ballot, White enthusiastically joined the campaign, even though he thought the platform "conservative to the point of reaction in its consideration of all social legislation excepting prohibition."[13] But prohibition became the central issue for White and a very emotional one. In speeches and in the press he attacked Democrat candidate Al Smith, a New York City Roman Catholic, with the same provincial bigotry he had condemned in the Ku Klux Klan. To the dismay of many of his friends—including his wife, his son, and his publisher George P. Brett, Jr.—he made a sorry spectacle of himself. Fortunately, he and Sallie spent part of the campaign in Europe.

With Hoover in the White House, Will once again had direct access to the office of the president and could influence federal patronage in Kansas. More important, he had influence in a policy area he had been interested in for some years: United States relations with Latin America. During his progressive years White had come to distrust the aims of American imperialism, in spite of TR's blustery big-stick diplomacy. In following the colorful career of his university fraternity brother Major-General Fred Funston, who had occasionally visited him in Emporia, he learned at first hand the problems of United States military intervention in underdeveloped countries. Funston, before his death in 1917, had been wounded and captured in Cuba, led the Army unit that in the Philippines hacked through jungles to seize the rebel leader Aguinaldo, and commanded American troops the several times President Wilson sent them into Mexico during the turmoil of the revolution. In the 1920s White was consistently critical of the Harding-Coolidge policy of Dollar Diplomacy, arguing in a 1927 letter to Senator Borah, chairman of the Senate Foreign Relations Committee, that we have "got to recognize that the flag does not follow the promoter or go to war with those countries which hold a different dollar view from ours."[14] Thus there was logic to Hoover's appointing White in February 1930 as one of five members of a commission to investigate conditions in Haiti. United States Marines had occupied that island since 1915 to protect American investments and maintain public peace, but such "peace" was greatly resented by many of the islanders because in 1929 the United States had to impose martial law to quell riots against its continued presence there. In the spirit of Hoover's new Good Neighbor Policy, the commissioners recommended democratic changes in the native government and gradual withdrawal of the Marines, which was provided for in a 1932 treaty.

After White returned from Haiti the great depression, triggered in the United States by the stock market crash of October 1929, engrossed much of his attention in the next few years, as it did that of most Americans. Believing at first that the economy was fundamentally sound and the economic setback merely a loss in confidence, Hoover reassured Americans that "prosperity is just around the corner." Unfortunately, he lacked the charisma to inspire people to turn that corner. And he was opposed philosophically to direct federal intervention in what he regarded as the private sphere. But as things got worse he had to take steps to support business and labor through the power of the state, with a program of public works, for instance, and with loans through the Reconstruction Finance Corporation, created in January 1932. But such measures were too little too late. Even White was moved to confess in a letter of December 1930 to James Kerney, a fellow member of the Haiti commission: "For a man who has high intentions and a noble purpose, our beloved President has a greater capacity for doing exactly the wrong thing at a nicely appointed right time than any man who ever polished his pants in the big chair at the White House."[15] Both to Hoover and to several of his close advisors who were White's personal friends he urged strong governmental measures and dramatic gestures of leadership, but to his chagrin that advice went unheeded.

White's frustration also increased because the Republican National Committee, though faced by world-wide economic disaster, refused to examine its staunch conservative traditions. He thus broke with the national party and worked hard in 1930 to help reelect the independent liberal Senator George Norris of Nebraska. In Kansas the Democrats defeated his Republican candidates for governor and U.S. senator, though his son was elected to the state legislature. He was especially discouraged by the strong race run by the independent candidate for governor, John R. Brinkley. He was a quack doctor who owned a private hospital and a powerful radio station at Milford, Kansas, which he used to promote goat-gland transplants for male rejuvenation. White regarded him as a demagogue potentially as dangerous as Governor Huey Long of Louisiana. White knew personally that many people were desperate to find a leader with quick solutions, because he served on both the president's and the governor's committees for unemployment relief and chaired the local program. Such frustration took its toll; in 1931, suffering from exhaustion and

Ménièr's syndrome, he spent six months away from the *Gazette* in New Mexico and Colorado.

Bull Moose among New Dealers

In 1932 he covered both national conventions, strongly criticized the Republican platform in his dispatches, yet during the campaign actively supported Hoover and a straight Republican ticket. Earlier, in a 1926 editorial reprinted in the collection *Forty Years on Main Street* (1937), White had bemoaned the nation's spiritless materialism and regretted that "No big figure looms on the horizon who is going to shock us into a realization of our deadly lethargy.... We have just got to grind along and develop our man, and it is a long, slow task calling for all our patience. How long, oh Lord, how long!" In a footnote in that collection, he mused, "Well six years brought the man! And when he came I someway did not 'get out and raise the flaming banner of righteousness.' But someone did!" (322). Alf Landon, the son of an old Bull Moose friend, ran for governor of Kansas with White's backing and survived the Democratic landslide, but only because Brinkley again ran as an independent and cut into the Democrat vote. Both the *Gazette* and its close ally the *Kansas City Star* editorially supported Landon and together led the attack on Brinkley, who represented "the organized moron minority, plus the despairing and disgruntled who knew better," according to White.[16] But such a description did not fit Franklin D. Roosevelt or the Democrats, and White knew that. He also knew Hoover had no chance. For in a letter to Harold Ickes, dated 14 July 1932, he commented about Roosevelt's acceptance speech at the Democrat convention: "I liked Roosevelt's speech. I was in the Hall and heard it. It seems to me the most important acceptance speech we have had for twenty years. And if Roosevelt can make good with it, nobody will be happier than I. I wonder if he will go the distance, that is all that bothers me."[17]

With FDR as president White downplayed the role of partisan gadfly to assume instead that of the puckish elderly "Sage of Emporia," who enthusiastically supported much of the early New Deal programs. Representing the most influential voice of moderately liberal mid-America, his editorials and comments expressed the hopes of many during the bleak days of the depression. He even had some personal influence with Roosevelt's "Brain Trust," for the new administration included friends from Progressive party years. Among them was Secretary of the Interior Ickes, whom he wrote in May 1933 with reference to FDR: "How do you account for him? Was I just fooled in him before the election, or has he developed? As Governor of New York, I thought he was a good, two-legged Governor of the type that used to flourish in the first decade under the influence of La Follette and Roosevelt. We had a lot of them, but they weren't Presidential size except Hiram Johnson, and I thought your President was one of these. Instead of which he developed magnitude and poise, more than all, power."[18] White understood the situation demanded a president of commanding stature who could lead the country out of hard times yet stay within the bounds of democracy. He recognized that FDR had that stature. Nevertheless, in 1936 he again confounded principles with loyalties and supported the Republican ticket.

On 31 May 1933 he and Sallie sailed to London where he reported the International Economic Conference for Wheeler's North American Newspaper Alliance, then they toured Europe for nearly four months, with White continuing his syndicated dispatches. Because he had always been interested in the Soviet experiment, they visited Russia, whose social structure he described with qualified sympathy. Then they traveled to Austria and Italy, where he interviewed Benito Mussolini. He avoided Germany, however, because of his hatred of the Nazis, whom he described presciently in a 1933 Armistice Day editorial as "paranoiac sadists."[19] During their last weeks in Europe the Whites knew they were coming home to the heartache of scandal, though they kept that news from a young traveling companion, for it involved her father and brother.

Perhaps the Whites' most intimate friends in Emporia were Mr. and Mrs. Warren Finney; the two families had been close for years and often vacationed together. In September 1933 Warren and his son Ronald were charged with forging more than a million dollars in Kansas municipal bonds and with looting the Fidelity State Bank, controlled by the elder Finney. They were found guilty and sentenced to long prison terms. The elder Finney then committed suicide.[20] It was a painful period for the Whites. Though Will himself was innocent of any prior knowledge, the scandal did involve several important state officials, one of whom was Kansas Attorney General Roland Boynton, White's cousin and protégé, who was impeached by the state legislature. White fought for him tenaciously because he believed him innocent, though inept, and believed the scandal and impeachment jeopardized his own reputation and long-established position in the state party. Boynton was exonerated, then White in order to demonstrate he was still a power in state politics worked hard in the Kansas campaigns of 1934, especially for the election of Clarence Beck of Emporia as attorney general and the re-election of Landon as governor.

Early in 1935 the *Kansas City Star* and the Stauffer newspaper chain started a presidential boom for Landon. Though White realized no Republican could beat FDR for a second term, he too backed Landon's bid for the nomination. His reasons were mixed. On one hand he believed him moderately progressive and hoped his candidacy would liberalize the national party. On the other, he had strong personal ties to Landon and the group around him, one being Sallie's brother-in-law Lacy Haynes, an editor of the *Star* and chief tactician to Landon. But White put politics behind him the winter of 1935–36 while he and Sallie toured the Far East. As a member of the board of trustees of the Rockefeller Foundation he represented it at the inauguration of the first president of the Philippines, then visited hospitals funded by it in that country and in China. When they returned to Emporia, he was pleased to find Landon the front runner for the nomination but disturbed by the number of conservatives gathering around him, especially William Randolph Hearst, whom he despised both as a journalist and as a political force. At the end of February he wrote Morris L. Ernst, a prominent New York City lawyer: "Hearst, to my notion, is the most vicious influence in American life—bar none. He is worse than Aimee McPherson, Father Coughlin, Huey Long, Cardinal O'Connell, Bishop Manning and Jim Reed all rolled in one."[21] When White went East that spring to attend a meeting of the American Society of Newspaper Editors, he campaigned for Landon but with developing misgivings. He also had misgivings about what he called FDR's "unconscious arrogance of conscious wealth" that White feared made him capable of abusing the vast power of the state. Thus he felt himself in a predicament rendered especially painful by the fact that he was a figure of trust to a large national audience.

When the conventions met, he reported them for his syndicate and served as the Kansas delegate to the Republican platform committee, but reluctantly and only at Landon's insistence. Even though he and Landon pushed for a somewhat liberal platform, Old Guard reactionaries controlled the party. The Republican campaign that fall acrimoniously attacked Roosevelt and the New Deal and depicted Landon as more conservative than he really was; in the election results Landon did not even carry Kansas. As much as possible White had kept away from the Republican national organization during that campaign. But he did not sit it out, though he undoubtedly wished to, for he wrote many letters and several newspaper features supporting Landon, plus interpretive articles for the *New York Times Magazine* and the *Saturday Evening Post*. Following the format of his earlier book, *Politics: The Citizen's Business*, he combined those two articles with some of his syndicated dispatches written during the convention, added the candidates' acceptance speeches and the party platforms, and asked Macmillan to issue them in September as the campaign handbook *What It's All About*. Though partisan the book was far from a puff.

White devoted the next two years to completing his second biography of Calvin Coolidge—but not all of his attention by any means. In the first months of 1937 he joined the fight against FDR's proposal to add up to six more justices to the U.S. Supreme Court to break its conservative block. White opposed the plan in national newspaper articles and in appeals to his friends in Congress. A strong libertarian, he believed the proposal would establish a dangerous precedent for tampering with the American system of checks and balances. Usually, White supported New Deal programs during Roosevelt's second term, as he did the first, though as a Republican he criticized what he saw as the president's manipulative administrative style. But because both men were tolerant partisans, they developed a mutual respect over the years that made possible White's important work in 1939–40 as chairman of two effective public relations committees to aid the Allies. For, like Roosevelt, he loathed fascism in its various guises, perceived the folly of isolationism, and watched in dismay and some confusion the coming of another world war in the late 1930s. But first he fought fascism at home.

After recovering from a second round of prostate surgery at the Mayo Clinic in the winter of 1937–38, he returned to a new outburst of bigotry in Kansas led by the Wichita revivalist Gerald B. Winrod, who was seeking the Republican nomination for U.S. Senate. Winrod was one of the most extreme of the native rightists fomenting hatred during those troubled times. Appalled that such a man could be the Republican candidate for U.S. senator from Kansas, White marshaled all his forces and helped defeat him in the primary. Winrod maintained a following, though, and stridently advocated fascism, attacking White and other liberals until imprisoned for sedition during World War II.

Once in such a fight, White always gave it his all, but in January 1938 he had turned seventy—an event celebrated by a large hometown birthday party which was featured in Fox Movietone News and *Life* and *Look* magazines.[22] The event was commemorated also in many newspaper columns and editorials across the nation. For years he had spoken out for small-town America. Before he could vote he was up to his neck in politics and stayed there. He had accumulated honorary degrees from Harvard, Columbia, Brown, Northwestern, and many smaller institutions. He supported many national public interest and charitable associations as a member or an officer. Indeed, according to David Hinshaw, White's charitable contributions over his lifetime totaled more than the estate he left.[23] For forty-three years he had been the foremost booster of Emporia, an active Rotarian who led the drives for a YMCA building and a civic auditorium and gave the town its fifty-acre Peter Pan Park in memory of his daughter. Now he wished to withdraw from the center of the fray. Aware of his advancing age, he had become reflective about changes in America during his lifetime and wanted to work on an autobiography. Before he started that project, though, he put together a series of three philosophically reminiscent lectures which he delivered at Harvard in April 1939. Macmillan issued them as *The Changing West: An Economic Theory about Our Golden West.* That was his last book published during his life, because international events interfered with the autobiography.

Ambivalent Interventionist

In 1935 when Italy invaded Ethiopia, White reflected the confusion of the time by forgetting his previous advocacy of internationalism and editorially favoring passage of the Neutrality Act. But after the Spanish Civil War between fascists and republicans began in 1936 and the Japanese invaded China in 1937, he realized strict neutrality was impossible in an industrialized world and supported international cooperation, short of war. Like FDR he understood American involvement in a world war was only a matter of time, but paradoxically, like many Americans, he could not accept the immediacy of war until it was thrust upon him. When it became clear early in 1939 that Hitler would not honor international agreements, Roosevelt sought congressional revision of the Neutrality Act to permit economic aid to Britain and France in case of war. But a powerful group of Senate isolationists, mostly Republicans, blocked the president's move. After Hitler invaded Poland on 1 September 1939, Roosevelt convened a special session of Congress to revise the Neutrality Act and repeal the arms embargo so that the Allied Powers could buy war equipment on at least a cash and carry basis. Much of the public favored the president's requests, but their support had to be rallied immediately and made known to Congress. Members of the Union for Concerted Peace Efforts, directed by Clark Eichelberger, decided an ad hoc committee led by a distinguished Midwesterner would best do that job. Secretary of State Cordell Hull recommended White, and after some urging he agreed to chair the Non-Partisan Committee for Peace through Revision of the Neutrality Law. He immediately went to New York City and during October frenetically directed the activities of that committee to mobilize support and pressure Congress. On 3 November Congress passed Roosevelt's requested revisions, against stiff isolationist opposition.

Events moved rapidly in Europe. Russia concluded a nonaggression pact with Germany just before Hitler invaded Poland, then Russia attacked Finland. White's son was in Europe as a war correspondent, and on Christmas Day broadcast for CBS a moving report from the Finnish front. White was deeply affected by his son's broadcast and his other reports and at the same time puzzled about what the United States should do, as was the president himself, who outlined for White in a long, confidential letter of 14 December the various alternatives facing the country and concluded: "Therefore, my sage old friend, my problem is to get the American people to think of conceivable consequences without scaring the American people into thinking that they are going to be dragged into this war."[24] That spring when Hitler launched his "blitzkrieg" through neutral Norway and Denmark, then the Low Countries and into France, White again hurried to New York City, this time to confer with Clark Eichelberger about creating the Committee to Defend America by Aiding the Allies. They agreed that it was needed and that their goal was to move public opinion toward granting more aid to Great Britain and France without going to war. On 17 May White sent telegrams from Emporia to prominent figures in the various areas of public life—

education, religion, politics, business and journalism—asking them to help him form the committee. Telegrams of acceptance soon poured into the *Gazette* office. White assumed the chairmanship, Eichelberger served as executive director, and six representative public figures made up the executive committee. They immediately began building sentiment for extending economic and military aid to the Allies, who really consisted only of Great Britain after France fell on 22 June. Soon the "White Committee" had local branches all over the country and was pressuring Congress to support Roosevelt's foreign policy through radio speeches, newspaper advertisements, rallies, and letter and telegraph campaigns.

That summer White, as usual, reported the national conventions for his syndicate. At the Republican convention in Philadelphia he supported the successful inclusion of a platform plank favoring aid "to all peoples fighting for liberty," then covered Wendell Willkie's successful bid for the nomination against several isolationist candidates. In Chicago at the Democrat convention, both he and Eichelberger joined others in urging the platform committee to adopt a plank favoring aid to the Allies, which they did. During the campaign White supported Willkie, mainly because of the third-term issue, though he continued to praise Roosevelt's foreign policy. In fact, just after the conventions, at the request of Roosevelt, he asked Willkie to support publicly the exchange of fifty desperately needed overage destroyers to England for some naval bases in this hemisphere. As liaison White was only partially successful: Willkie did not commit the Republicans to that transfer, but he also did not make foreign policy a campaign issue. That in itself was a patriotic act, because the debate over isolation or intervention smoldered through the campaign. In September some prominent Republican conservatives, in opposition to the "White Committee," formed the America First Committee to mobilize isolationist opinion and began a vituperative crusade against FDR's foreign policy.

In addition to his work for the committee, White had political matters at home to take care of. He worked for the reelection of his political ally Governor Payne Ratner and campaigned across the state in support of a constitutional amendment setting up a state civil service system he had sponsored for years. Though the "White Committee" was officially nonpartisan, many members wanted the organization to oppose congressional isolationists running for reelection, nearly all Republican. Undoubtedly, that step would have been effective, but White vetoed the idea, partially because of his own bewildering political loyalties, to the dismay of the aggressive wing of the committee. After the elections the policy-making members of the committee met in New York and, together with White, decided to advocate in general terms repeal of the Neutrality Act and adoption of some form of the lend-lease program soon to be announced by FDR. But after his return to Emporia, White worried about the more "provocative" stance the committee had taken. On reflection it seemed to him they had significantly outdistanced the prevailing opinion of his middle-class constituency. When he learned that Roy Howard, head of the large Scripps-Howard chain, planned to attack the committee's new policy in his newspapers, he wrote to him disavowing any change, then allowed Howard to print the letter. That caused such indignation within the committee that White, realizing he no longer represented it, resigned as active chairman 3 January and honorary chairman 3 April 1941.

Prophet with Honor

His own reluctance to move the country closer to war, his age, his own and Sallie's deteriorating health, and the many abusive personal attacks by extreme isolationists had taken their toll. On doctor's orders he and Sallie left for Arizona, where he believed she suffered a light stroke; her health remaining frail, they went to the Mayo Clinic where they were told she suffered from nervous exhaustion and that both needed to slow down and rest more. Yet during 1941 White closely followed the Battle of Britain, Hitler's invasion of Russia, and the German expansion of submarine warfare in the Atlantic. In *Gazette* editorials he vigorously supported Roosevelt's foreign policy and attacked the isolationism of his own party. In fact, in an editorial the day after the Japanese bombed Pearl Harbor he laid the blame squarely upon the congressional Republicans who voted against military preparedness and aid to Great Britain: "We are at war now instead of later because the Republican leadership in Congress fooled the Japanese into thinking they could attack a divided country. The shame of that vote is obvious to all."[25] Still, he continued a local Republican boss and in 1942, even though he wanted time to work on his autobiography, he buckled on his armor once again for the state primary fights. In spite of his age and a long-standing diabetic condition, his vitality and spirit were irrepressible:

that summer, for instance, he wrote his long-time friend novelist Edna Ferber,

I get as much copy up as anyone around the shop, and of course have my finger in a lot of local pies. Just now I am helping to nominate a governor and am busier than a man falling out of a balloon without a parachute. But it would be pretty terrible not to be part of things. . . . I am state chairman of the War Bond drive and one of the national directors of the Red Cross and what with one thing and another, manage to keep the moss off the north side and the mildew off my brain and the cobwebs out of my eyes.[26]

Though his state candidates won in 1942, White found little comfort on the national scene in the reelection of so many isolationists and in the continued conservative stance of the Republican party. He looked to the 1944 presidential campaign with foreboding and feared a future repeat of postwar reaction. But the resiliency of FDR as a wartime president amazed him and he was unabashed in his editorial praise: "Biting nails—good hard bitter Republican nails—we are compelled to admit that Franklin Roosevelt is the most unaccountable and on the whole the most enemy-baffling president the United States has ever seen."[27] Several times early in 1943 he and Sallie traveled East to Washington and New York City where he attended conferences, met with politicians, and conferred with the other Book-of-the-Month Club judges. But in April while in New York they both came down with the flu and spent their fiftieth wedding anniversary in Roosevelt Hospital instead of New Mexico as planned. His flu turned into pneumonia and after they were able to travel they went home and then to Colorado to recuperate. But he never really bounced back; at his cabin in the Rockies that summer he told an interviewer "I've got lead in my pants and I love to sit down and look nature squarely in the face without batting an eye."[28] Still, he did cast his eyes from time to time at the national scene and continued to write an occasional editorial and syndicated commentary.

Feeling worse that fall, he underwent surgery at the Mayo Clinic and found he had cancer. After lingering a few months, he died 29 January 1944. Among the hundreds of press eulogies and private messages of condolence, FDR's telegram to Sallie expressed succinctly the sense of loss felt by much of the nation: "The newspaper world loses one of its wisest and most beloved editors in the death of William Allen White. He made the Emporia *Gazette* a national institution.

As a writer of terse, forcible and vigorous prose, he was unsurpassed. He ennobled the profession of journalism which he served with such unselfish devotion through more than two score years. To me his passing brings a real sense of personal loss. . . ."[29] White's son edited the unfinished autobiography, which appeared in 1946 and won a Pulitzer prize, an appropriate tribute to the story of his life.

Chapter Three

A Kansas Publicist: Journalism

Today we remember William Allen White as America's most extraordinary small-town newspaper editor and publicist of the first decades of this century. Together with the somewhat earlier "Marse Henry" Watterson of the *Louisville Courier-Journal* and the contemporaneous Josephus Daniels of the *Raleigh News and Observer*, he was one of the last of our nationally known personal journalists. By the 1920s he had become generally recognized as the "public voice of grassroots democracy," the outstanding editorial spokesman of liberal Midwestern middle-class public opinion. In 1923, for example, Oswald G. Villard, editor of the *Nation*, declared in *Some Newspapers and Newspaper-Men*, an analytical critique of the American press, that "there is no Middle Western editor of national prominence between the Mississippi and 'the Coast' except Mr. White."[1] Yet his editorials appeared in a small Kansas daily that in the 1920s had a circulation of only five or six thousand and mostly reported the affairs of a country town with a population of about 12,000. Paradoxically, by means of that paper's editorial column he strode forth as an outspoken progressive who impressed his ebullient personality and independent views upon the country at large.

White did that during the very years that brought such profound changes to newspaper publishing that personal journalism and the independent editor had virtually disappeared, from the dailies at least. The sensational mass appeal of yellow and jazz journalism; the rise of heavily capitalized, business-oriented chains; the increased importance of monopolistic press associations and feature syndicates; the development of display advertising in conjunction with regional and national accounts; and the expensive technological transformation of printing processes all doomed the small, locally owned newspaper and made conglomerates and big-city, big-circulation journalism the trend of the times. Joseph Pulitzer, defending his use of sensationalism in building the circulation of his pace-setting *New York World*, argued that "if a newspaper is to be of real service to the public it must have a big circulation, first because its news and comment must reach the largest number of people, second because circulation means advertising, and advertising means money, and money means independence."[2] The *Emporia Gazette* stands in the annals of American journalism as a notable exception.

But Pulitzer was right in the main. White created his national audience not by editing a small-town newspaper but by writing for mass-circulation magazines and nation-wide syndicates. After he established that audience, then he spoke to it by means of the *Gazette's* editorial page, but his words reached out only when copied by other newspapers from the daily edition or from a four-page weekly that carried the editorials and some local news with minimal advertising. Of course his editorials were frequently reprinted, or at least cited, because his views were good copy, partly due to his national reputation, and partly to his own cleverness and style. Though he adroitly acted the role of simple country editor, in actuality he was a sophisticated journalist who learned early how to upstage others and capture attention. A reporter for the *New York Times*, in commenting on White's bare-bones campaign for governor in 1924, asked rhetorically: "What need of campaign literature for a candidate whose talk is such rattling good copy that all the wires tingle to broadcast him? 'I don't ask editorial support,' he says, while all his independent fellow-editors rally to his side, 'What I want is to be news, first page stuff. As a mere editorial writer I know that the head liner is the real power of the press.'"[3] Calvin H. Lambert, city editor for the *Gazette* in the 1920s, remembered an example of that when reminiscing about his years with the paper: during White's controversy with Governor Henry Allen over the railway shopman strike, "a friend tipped off Mr. White of his impending arrest. That afternoon, he asked me to take him for a ride in the country. We rode and rode, going nowhere in particular. At 4 o'clock he pulled out his watch and remarked: 'We can go back now, so I can get arrested.' He had deliberately taken the trip so the news story would break for the morning papers, which would give him much better publicity."[4]

Judged against small-town middle-class standards, White by age forty was well-to-do. He had used his magazine fees and book royalties to put the *Gazette* on a profitable basis and to begin investing in local real estate. If Pulitzer was right, that money means independence, then editor White during much of his tenure could afford independence. In the *Autobiography* he mentions he paid his own

expenses in 1919 when speaking for the League of Nations, then in
an aside he comments:

I mention this fact not because it indicates any high moral principles but
because it was smart. Nearly a quarter of a century before, as a poor young
newspaperman, I let Cy Leland give me a hundred dollars for my expenses on a trip to Washington. Afterwards he boasted he had bought
me. On both my trips to Europe under Red Cross auspices I paid my
own railroad fare, steamship fare, hotel bills; and I have never gone
on any political mission that I did not pay my own expenses.... One sur-
renders his freedom while he is in service and his right afterwards to
change his mind and criticize or even denounce the cause he has espoused
if it goes wrong or if he discovers that it is making mistakes. In politics,
a man must pay for his freedom with his own checkbook. (577–78)

Yet White was not truly free. He was able to adhere to a high standard of newspaper ethics, but his loyalties were imprisoned by the
one-party system of Kansas politics and by a puzzling set of political
friendships. Nor could he strike off entirely the mental shackles of
his region, class, and time, which were to form many of his attitudes.
In his eyes he may have been his own man, but in the eyes of the
public he was a captive everyman—a Progressive Republican, Midwestern, middle-class, small-town everyman. That was his strength and
his weakness.

Since 1895 White's foremost concern was the business of editing
a small county-seat daily. His many other activities—national and state
politics, literature, social commentary—generated out of this central
interest. He knew his *Emporia Gazette* existed only insofar as it was
a good, well-managed local newspaper. So the most intimate part of
him was the small-town editor who shopped ostentatiously at local
stores to trade out advertising accounts, knew at least the family
names of most folks in town, and kept abreast of neighborhood
changes throughout his sales territory. He had no delusions of gran-
deur about his circulation or market and unabashedly cultivated rural
community correspondents with their "News from Neosho Rapids" or
"Americus Doings" and paid them with subscriptions to the *Saturday
Evening Post.* Likewise, he recognized the humorous familiarity of
his town and headed the letters-to-the-editor column "The Wailing
Place." Even during the busiest periods of his life he wrote two- or
three-line items gathered from his walks down Commercial Street,

and Sallie phoned in social items daily. His two children attended the public schools, and the family took in the cultural events scheduled by the two colleges. Editor White knew Emporia by the back, from its down-at-the-heels South End to the country club North End, from the company-built family quarters the Santa Fe scattered along its right-of-way for its Mexican gandy dancers to the "Colored Section" northeast along the embankment of the M.K.&T. railroad track. Emporia was Will White's town, though its populace sometimes did not think so.

White worked on newspapers for fifty-eight years; over those years he experienced the transformation of small-town journalism from a craft into a profession and then a business. By 1920 the days were gone when a young printer could come to town with a "shirttail full of type" and a few hundred dollars and start a newspaper. Drastic technological and economic changes had made that impossible. When White bought the *Gazette* in 1895, the printing equipment consisted of a water-run cylinder press, several cases of type, three composing stones, and a lead roller for pulling proofs. There were about 600 subscribers, many in arrears. In 1899 he bought new brevier type but changed in 1902 to a linotype and in 1903 secured Associated Press bulletin service, a "pony report" of about 3,000 words. In 1905 with over 2,000 subscribers he added another linotype and a Duplex web press with a folder. Sometime in those early years he bought several small job presses. In 1915 he added yet another linotype and in 1919 a Ludlow advertisement setter and a stereotyping outfit. In 1920 he expanded his news coverage by contracting for the full AP telegraph wire service to supplant the morning summary phoned to a stenographer from the AP Kansas City office which had itself replaced the pony report; circulation was nearly 5,000.

In a 1935 editorial White commemorated fifty years in journalism and remarked that when he bought the *Gazette* he could do everything he asked everyone else to do: "I could set type, put the paper to press, feed the press, kick the jobber, set the meager advertising that was used in those days, keep the books, solicit the advertising, take charge of the circulation, deliver the papers, solicit subscribers and run the bank account, such as it was." But now when he went into the backshop, "instead of being familiar with every process and being able to do every mechanical thing necessary to print *The Gazette*, I can do practically nothing, though my hands retain their one-time printer's skill."[5] Thus, he observed elsewhere, in the first decades of this century "journalism was ceasing to be a profession and was becoming a business and an industry."[6]

After he matured as a newspaper man, White spoke out against the press limitations implicit in those changes and attempted to enhance professionalism by example and criticism. He was both angered and saddened by the inevitable movement toward standardization because it removed personality from journalism. In a 1939 article for *Collier's* entitled "How Free Is the Press?" he paid tribute to the passing of the old era: " 'The Press' means a substantial investment today, a solid business institution—in short, property. The gay and insouciant editor, fleet of foot and swift of wing, who kept his position liquid by the insignificance of his investment today is an old man's dream. The old editor, horse whipped, shot at, sued for libel, has passed out of our civilization with the king's fool and the minnesinger, the jousting knight and the chimney sweep."[7] When Frank A. Munsey, businessman turned magazine publisher turned newspaper consolidator, died in 1925, White expressed his feelings about brokerage journalism in a famous terse obituary: "Frank Munsey, the great publisher, is dead. Frank Munsey contributed to the journalism of his day the talent of a meat packer, the morals of a money changer and the manners of an undertaker. He and his kind have about succeeded in transforming a once noble profession into an eight per-cent security. May he rest in trust!"[8]

On the other hand, if a publisher through monopoly or huge circulation imposed too much personality on his region, White also protested. Colonel Robert R. McCormick, owner of the *Chicago Tribune*, was a strong advocate of freedom of the press but ignored its concomitant responsibilities by outrageously editorializing news columns in the late 1930s with ultraconservative, isolationist opinions. White disagreed firmly with most of those opinions, but he objected even more to McCormick's methods, regarding the *Tribune* in 1942, after the start of the war, as "potentially the most dangerous newspaper in the United States" because of its news ethics.[9] And he had nothing but contempt for yellow journalism, claiming it pandered slavishly to unfortunate millions of moron morality and intelligence.[10] Early in his career he wrote John S. Phillips, then in charge of McClure's newspaper syndicate, cautioning him not to negotiate on his behalf with New York City's yellow press: "I would rather starve to death than to write for the New York *World*, or the New York *Journal*. Heaven knows I need the money bad enough; but I do not need it that bad."[11] For the rest of his life he refused to sell a word to any of William R. Hearst's papers.

White received his first meaningful lessons in professional ethics while working under Colonel Nelson at the *Star*. Nelson was one of the great among Midwestern publishers, for he ran a responsible, honest newspaper in a flamboyant age of boodle. Though competing against such rivals as the deeply yellow *Kansas City Post*, owned by the infamous Denver team of Harry H. Tammen and Fred G. Bonfils, the *Star* kept to its even tenor of conservative makeup and high ideals. From Nelson, for instance, White took his editorial vow against holding political office.[12] But he did not graduate from the *Star* with a full set of ethical credentials; they had to evolve over the years. In 1885 when he hired on as a printer's devil at the *El Dorado Republican*, most country editors could not afford to be nice about business ethics. Usually county-seat towns had a couple of half-starved newspapers started and supported by rival local factions. In hustling for a meager living opposing editors lavished encomiums or heaped abuse upon friend and foe, as determined by their papers' supporters or in not very covert blackmail of prominent citizens. Much later, when writing about the ethics of advertising for the *Atlantic Monthly*, White recalled buying a new set of type when he was assistant editor of the *Republican* from the advertising agency of N. W. Ayer & Son by contracting to carry questionable patent medicine ads for several years.[13] Since that was standard *modus operandi*, few questioned it.

But after he bought the *Gazette* he began to question such methods. From the first he refused to sling mud at his rivals and concentrated instead upon gathering local news. He kept references to himself and his activities to a minimum and omitted personalities from whatever political fights the *Gazette* took part in.[14] Eventually he refused ads for dubious patent medicines, quack doctors, unlisted mining stocks, liquor, and tobacco. He printed only the court findings in divorce cases and banned resolutions of respect and husbands' notices of refusal to pay the wife's bills. He did not publicize the names of first offenders in police court but otherwise never deleted a name or suppressed a news story in the interest of friendship, observing in a 1903 editorial that "when an editor begins monkeying with his conscience, stretching his rule to shield his friends or to punish his enemies, he is lost."[15] He stressed accuracy and style in reporting the news, maintained a high standard of civic responsibility on the editorial page, and severely limited syndicated filler, omitting comics until his staff wore him down on that issue. Thus the *Gazette* came to exemplify the archetypal high-minded small-town newspaper. If a newspaper is but the lengthened shadow of its editor, the *Gazette* also exemplified Will A. White.

He was a good boss, accessible and fair to his employees, though at the same time demanding high standards of them. So long as they upheld those standards, he allowed them considerable freedom in the columns of the paper. Walt Mason, for example, was a die-hard Republican conservative and a frequent *Gazette* editorialist, which sometimes confused subscribers. During the 1912 presidential campaign he inveighed against Bull Moose madness, refused to stay at the office, and rabidly supported Taft, yet White allowed him to publish what he pleased in his own column.[16] T. F. McDaniel, a *Gazette* employee for more than forty years, recalled that when White vehemently attacked the Ku Klux Klan in 1924 one of his staff was an influential local Kluxer: "The boss knew this and the employee knew that he knew and both got along fine, each respecting the other's opinions."[17]

Because of the national reputation of White as a demanding but fair editor, many young staff members over the years "graduated" from the *Gazette*, the "White School of Journalism," to successful newspaper careers elsewhere. For seven years White was a member of the Advisory Board of the prestigious Graduate School of Journalism at Columbia University and in 1938 was elected president of the American Society of Newspaper Editors. The name of his paper became the byword for upstanding personal journalism. But neither his personal qualities as an editor nor the unimpeachable standards of his newspaper was the real reason for the *Gazette*'s fame. For there were a number of country newspapers throughout the United States just as clean and straight. What made it a national institution was White's prestige as a writer of editorials.

Editorialist: *The Editor and His People* and *Forty Years on Main Street*

The editorial is an amorphous literary genre, if it can even be called a genre. Whether argument or exposition or both, its movement is discursive, in either sense of that adjective; its subject is any thing under the sun, or the sun itself; and its tone varies from ribald to stodgy. Like all journalism it is ephemeral, despite the prestige of writer or journal, despite the topic. The historian-journalist Allan Nevins in *American Press Opinion* pointed to the evanescence of the form when he wrote: "The editor, no matter how distinguished, writes in water; his page is a palimpsest, on which he expends all his talents, wit, learning and judgment for the day alone, to be erased with the next sun.... At best, some small fragments—a few biting phrases, a fulmination which perhaps accidentally has made a distinct mark in history—are kept alive."[18] White is lucky in that regard. Three of his editorials—"What's the Matter with Kansas?" "Mary White," and "To an Anxious Friend"—are still reprinted and by that criterion alive. And more than 600 were saved from the near oblivion of the microfilmed files of the *Gazette*, available in less than half a dozen libraries, by two collections: *The Editor and His People*, compiled by Helen O. Mahin (1924) and *Forty Years on Main Street*, edited by Russell H. Fitzgibbon (1937).

In the 1920s Helen Mahin was an instructor in the School of Journalism at the University of Kansas; with White's permission she began a short compilation of his editorials for classroom use. That project grew into a book containing 266 editorials. White did not concern himself with selection, but he did influence format and wrote the continuity. Thus he contributed a preface and brief introspective introductions to the ten topical sections, and an occasional footnote. Each section is ordered chronologically. Russell Fitzgibbon, a professor of political science at Hanover College in Indiana in 1936–37, put together an almost entirely different selection. Of the 370 editorials included by him only seventeen repeat Mahin's earlier collection. Fitzgibbon used thirteen topical categories to group his choices, with the editorials in each category arranged "logically" rather than chronologically. He wrote a general introduction to the book and a preface to each section. Frank C. Clough, long-time assistant editor of the *Gazette*, contributed a foreword. Though White supplied a few explanatory footnotes, he was otherwise uninvolved with this compilation.[19]

Both collections trace White's growth as a man, from the shrill young reactionary to the mellow old sage, and document his reputation as a maverick. For he lived by Emerson's dictum that a foolish consistency is the hobgoblin of little minds. Or, as he phrased it in a 1923 editorial:

Of all the cowardly, of all the wobbly pussyfooters, the man who is afraid of his own record is the worst. The thing that should govern a man is not what he once said but the truth as he sees it. A man who ignores the truth because he once failed to see the truth is probably a fool and never saw the truth. For facts change and with changing facts come changing conclusions. Yesterday's truth is tomorrow's error. Only the man who is wise enough to know this has a hold on truth. Consistency is a paste jewel that only cheap men cherish.[20]

When Oswald G. Villard, a well-known editor himself, reviewed *Forty Years on Main Street* in the *Nation*, he reacted to it with the same kind of persiflage (one of White's favorite words) its author was noted for. Referring to the attitudinal kaleidoscope of the collection, he proclaimed "of all the American liberals Bill White of Emporia is the most pernickety, perverse, pernicious, and periodic. He is the most often mistaken, inconsistent, unwise, short-sighted, percipient, emotional, banal, self-righteous, self-critical, partisan and independent, generally maddening, and altogether lovable conservative in the entire country."[21] Like G. B. Shaw's Sir Andrew Undershaft, White lived a life of purposeful service following the motto "Unshamed!"

But we must grant any editorialist the right to change his mind because, paradoxically, the one constant in human affairs is change. In White's case those changes followed a fairly consistent move from conventional Republican conservativism to an independent liberalism uneasily constrained by time, place, and circumstances. More than that we should not expect, for as White himself once remarked, "About all the public has a right to ask of an editorial writer is an honest mind, a kindly heart ribbed with courage, and such intelligence as the day's work may bring to him. In the nature of things, comment on the news while it is news must be a guess. News is a chameleon."[22]

As an editorialist he wrote with gusto, clarity, and humanity, though at first he sometimes omitted humanity. He was a provincial and callow partisan when he bought the *Gazette.* He had read the works of Emerson and Whitman with enthusiasm and at the university had been influenced by Professor James H. Canfield, a social democrat; nevertheless, in the everyday workaday world of young editor White social and political liberalism was embodied in desperately impoverished Populist farmers whom he saw as self-interested free silver advocates or worse. Without thinking much about it, then, he supported plutocracy as a way of life and enlisted in its army. When he wrote "What's the Matter with Kansas?" he had not been farther East than St. Louis, had not met the group of writers associated with Way and Williams in Chicago or the *McClure's* group in New York City nor had met Teddy Roosevelt in Washington, D.C. Only then did he question the assumptions behind conservative Republican politics in Kansas.

As his horizons lifted, his editorial topics did too; he turned from strident, Babbitt-like boosts for his hometown to more quizzically philosophical observations about the passing scene; he shifted his eyes from the arena of politics to notice the much larger stage of human social behavior. Moreover, his tone changed; he came to view people and events with infinitely more sophistication and tolerance. In a 1901 editorial about the assassination of President McKinley by Leon Czolgosz, a native-born anarchist of Polish-German ancestry, he declared with misdirected chauvinistic fervor: "Millions of Polaks and Hunkies and Italians, the very scum of European civilization, have been shipped into America to fill mines and furnaces and replace honest, well-paid, intelligent, conscientious American labor. This greed of money makers has filled America with human vermin; liberty with them means license."[23] By contrast, after seventeen years of involvement in national and even world affairs, he had the vision to see that "today in Russia, all uninformed, all blind, all mad and tremendously stupid, stands a new man in the world. The worker. This will be his century. . . . The leisure class brought beauty into the world at a terrible price to human progress. The middle class brought efficiency into the world. And the poor have paid more than their share for it. The prize in the hands of labor is peace—peace with justice! And all the world must help to pay. . . ."[24] In an 1896 editorial against United States military involvement in Cuba he declared with isolationist bigotry: "The people of Cuba are mongrels with no capacity for self government. If they throw off the tyranny of Spain, they would have a tyrant of their own. They are a yellow legged knife-sticking treacherous outfit, and the people of the United States have nothing in common with them."[25] By 1922 he recognized such ethnocentrism for what it was: "the white man does not think of his dark-skinned fellow traveler on the planet as a human companion. The white man considers any colored man—black, brown, red, yellow, or maroon—as an animal. The anthropological conceit of the white man is ponderous, unbelievable, vastly amusing to the gods."[26]

While both collections trace the maturation of Will A. White, they also demonstrate over and over the grounds for his reputation as a phrasemaker. His editorials were informal, even breezy, replete with colloquialisms and slang but under tight control, with a wide and exact vocabulary in ready reserve unencumbered by slavish adherence to the rule of monosyllabic simplicity. In a 1910 editorial he observed, "The first duty of a writer is to make his meaning clear, and when he chooses words it is with that end in view, and not with an ambition to economize in letters and syllables."[27] David Hinshaw, a former *Gazette* employee and a nationally known publicist, asserted in his reminiscent biography *A Man from Kansas* that White wrote his *Gazette* editorials in two styles, one addressed to the home folks—loose, slangy, and locally topical—and one intended for his national audience—more formal, tighter, with broader references.[28] That is not noticeable in the two collections, which include many editorials about local matters as well as national. While they do indicate he tailored style to weight of subject somewhat, they also demonstrate he did not alter it to the presumed size of audience. His longtime assistant editor Frank Clough reported in his brief biography that if White had the opportunity, he copyedited several proofs of an editorial but did that for all, regardless of topic.[29] For Emporia was to him a microcosm of the nation and in some respects the world; he believed that what he wrote about his town and its people was just as true elsewhere and potentially as worthwhile.

Often other newspapers picked up one of his local editorials because of its humor. He had a rambunctious sense of humor that kept him from taking his subjects or, for that matter, himself with dour seriousness. He usually viewed events and personages of the day with his head cocked askew. And he was funny precisely because of that mildly ironic way of seeing them, for he was a humorist, not a wit or a comic or a satirist. He did not use irony as a heavy weapon of attack; instead he was whimsical, self-denigrating but knowledgeable, and usually upbeat because he did not forget to add a splash or two from the jug of human kindness when mixing up his recipes for the day. As a humorist he looked at the world not quite from his fellow humorist Will Rogers' perspective of a sly, knowing naiveté and certainly not from his friendly opponent H. L. Mencken's vistas of brash iconoclasm, but rather from the down-home standpoint of casual familiarity, bringing the pompous to size with the wholesome irreverence of rural democracy not far removed from frontier times.

As rhetorical techniques he used the standard devices of understatement and overstatement with amusing effect, but his foremost stock-in-trade was surprise, the assumption of an unusual attitude or the use of unexpected diction: the apt biblical allusion, the homely figure of speech, the outrageous colloquialism, the original and striking epithet. For example, he once described the reputation of the wife in a widely reported Topeka divorce case as "looking like an unbleached slop bucket the day after the stovepipe fell down in the kitchen."[30] In editorial support of Rudyard Kipling's poetic assertion in 1899 of a white man's burden as part of the natural order, White wrote, "Kipling is the best poet for 'draft and general purposes' in the world today and anyone who denies this statement is a lumpy jawed, white livered, lopeared idiot who doesn't know enough to do light housework in a livery stable."[31] When members of the Progressive party wanted to run White for governor in 1914, he squelched that idea by writing

nix on Willyum Allen. The Gazette's nose is hard and cold on the proposition to make him governor. He is a four-flusher, a ring-tailed, rip-snorting hell-raiser, and a grandstander. He makes a big noise. He yips and kyoodles around a good deal, but he is everlastingly and preeminently N.G. as gubernatorial timber—full of knots, warts, woodpecker holes, and rotten spots. He would have the enmity of more men who have walked the plank politically than any other man in Kansas, and his candidacy would issue an irrevocable charter in Kansas for the Progressive party to be the official minority report world without end.... It may be that the Progressive party needs a goat, but the demand doesn't require a Billy-goat! Now is the time for all good men to come to the aid of the party. But this man White is a shoulder-galled, sore-backed, hamstrung, wind-broken, string-halted, stump sucking old stager who, in addition to being no good for draft and general purposes, has the political bots, blind-staggers, heaves, pink eye and epizootic.[32]

No surprise: he killed beyond resurrection any talk of a draft. In a sympathetic comment on an unflattering photo run by a number of newspapers of the aging Bryan napping on a hot afternoon, White observed any man was vulnerable and facetiously suggested doing the same to any film idol we wished to supplant: "About three o'clock we would make a flashlight unprefaced by an announcement, send out a few copies of the picture, and sit down for a month for results. Then when the laughter began to subside, we would breeze into the market with our young and unknown meal ticket with less competition than Noah's Greater Combined Circus and Wild West."[33] Similar to Noah's numbers, of course, are further examples of editor White's humor; a final sample here is his whimsical observation, "A Cuban poet with a name like a college yell, Gustave Sanchez Galarraga—and may the spelling of it be on the proof reader's hands— declares that he has a 'romantic soul.' As if that were strange! Who has not? One of God's precious gifts to man, one of the proofs of our kinship with the divine, is the romantic soul of us; individually, as poor worms of the dust, living in waste places and treading drab or even shady, sordid paths, we choose the rainbows, listen for the fairies, hope for the prize, and look even for our lost crystal slippers."[34]

In this troubled century White earned much of his respect as an editorialist not because he entertained but because he taught. He marched to the beat of his own drum, relying on his own hard-won homespun philosophy of life and imparting it with sincerity, if not consistency. He was no cynic, no pollyanna: he was a tempered optimist. He too listened for the fairies. In his maturity his editorial stance was based on an aggregate of idealism, compassion, sentiment, and what he once described as "intelligent discontent." Philosophically, he was a melioristic humanist. A succinct example of that attitude is in a 1913 editorial explaining his policy not to report local scandal:

The sad stories of life, unless they are forced into publicity by court record, or by some crisis of a public event, are not, as a rule, good reading. Lives of men and women are not always pleasant. The good Lord, looking down on us, sees much that must make him smile and sigh at the perversity of his handiwork. For the ways of a serpent on a rock and an eagle in the air are not the only queer things in this queer world. But queer things are not important. The important things of life are its kindnesses, its nobility, its self-denials, its great renunciations.[35]

As a widely reprinted editorialist and humorist White reminded the nation of those important things of life, hence the half-jocular title he acquired in early middle age, "The Sage of Emporia."

Magazine Free-Lancer

During the heyday of mass-circulation magazines White was a prolific free-lance contributor. Over his lifetime he sold hundreds of pieces of all sorts and lengths to nearly forty different nationally known magazines or journals and to many others of only limited circulations. At first many of these contributions were short stories but later submissions were entirely nonfiction, from light to serious, from brief commentary to carefully prepared feature articles. They ranged in subject matter from "The Golden Rule" in the prestigious *Atlantic Monthly* to "The Country Newspaper" in *Harper's Magazine* to "Beefsteak as I Prepare It" in *Better Homes and Gardens*. For much of his life the weekly *Collier's* and *Saturday Evening Post* were his most consistent markets, but from 1897 to 1912 he also wrote extensively for the monthly *McClure's* and then the *American Magazine*. He became known, in fact, as one of the *McClure's* group and has been identified with them by some social historians as a muckraker, though in truth he does not fit that category. For he was like his fellow contributor Finley Peter Dunne, who commented on current affairs in the guise of Mr. Martin Dooley, an Irish saloon keeper from Chicago's South Side. Both had grown up with Gilded Age politics and neither could work up the proper sense of astonishment and outrage which provided the undertone to the work of most of the muckrakers. And, too, White was a humorist and an incurable optimist, clearly recognized as such by his fellows. When the group deserted Sam McClure in 1906 to buy their own magazine, Dunne wrote a letter of explanation to President Roosevelt; in it he mentioned that "William Allen White has promised to take up the 'merry sunshine' work in a more serious and effective fashion, and I look to him to save our countrymen from the suicide which is the logical consequence of believing all we read now-a-days."[36]

In that era of the muckrakers White wrote some of his best remembered articles and developed a specialty and a technique of reporting that he carried over to his three book-length biographies. These articles were critical-analytical personality sketches of prominent politicians, irrespective of party. In them he attempted to explain American politics by describing those most conspicuously involved—presidents, unsuccessful presidential candidates, party bosses, big-city machine politicians. They are studies of the pragmatics of politics and thus are in the spirit, if not the tone, of the early muckrakers—of Ida Tarbell, Lincoln Steffens, Samuel Hopkins Adams, Ray Stannard Baker. Actually, the best of the muckrakers were simply good reporters who attempted earnestly to discover the forces involved in the rapid industrialization and urbanization of American life and the motives and ethics of those forces. The obvious popularity of such reporting, which *McClure's* identified first in its January 1903 issue as representing a trend, demonstrated that a large appetite existed for exposure journalism. Somewhat unconsciously *McClure's* had tapped the spirit of reform bubbling up in the nation at that time. *Collier's, Everybody's, Arena, Cosmopolitan,* and others immediately followed *McClure's* lead. But after Hearst bought *Cosmopolitan* in 1905 and published David Graham Phillips' lurid "The Treason of the Senate," much exposure journalism became self-consciously sensational and its importance waned. But that did not affect the market for White's free-lance contributions because he was never pigeon-holed a muckraker by magazine editors or readers.

Masks in a Pageant. In 1928 White rewrote many of his magazine sketches from various years to publish them as the fourteen portraits of his book *Masks in a Pageant,* at least so he implies in the introduction, stating:

These chapters are for the most part a reporter's notes elaborated. To illustrate: In 1900, William Jennings Bryan was running for President. *McClure's Magazine* asked me to write an article about Bryan. Since then, as a reporter, I have seen Bryan in every National Democratic Convention where he has appeared, or where his name was presented. I came to know him well. I have written many articles about him—always I have written as a reporter. From these articles the chapter about Bryan was prepared. Similarly, the chapters about Mark Hanna, Senator Platt, Richard Croker, have grown from articles written as news—if what is called a timely magazine article is news.[37]

In truth White did not significantly revise the text of articles he used for seven of the portraits in this book and as a result we have ready access to some of his best-known magazine sketches and can thereby discern in part his qualities as a magazine writer. For other chapters he did edit the original articles thoroughly by cutting and rewriting to update his perspective and provide continuity. And for all the articles he changed format by chopping the originals into short chapters under descriptive headings and occasionally into shorter paragraphs, especially the earlier ones, to conform to a more modern copy style. To give structure to his compilation he grouped them under traditional categories of English history: "The Old Kings" are Tammany boss Richard Croker and New York state boss Senator Platt; "The Early Stuarts," presidents Benjamin Harrison, Cleveland, and McKinley; "The Two Warwicks," Senator Hanna and presidential aspirant Bryan; "The Great Rebellion" features presidents Roosevelt, Taft, and Wilson; "The Restoration" brings presidents Harding and Coolidge; and "The Young Princes of Democracy" are New York Governor Al Smith and Chicago Mayor William H. Thompson. Despite such tinkering the text of half of the sketches of the book are close to prototype.[38]

Early in 1900 Sam McClure commissioned White to write a series of studies of conspicuous contemporary political figures. When the magazine published the first, the one on Bryan, in July 1900, it announced their nature and rationale in a prefatory note:

The characters to be presented in this series have been chosen irrespective of the political sympathies of either Mr. White or of the editors of *McClure's*, and solely because of the position they occupy in the mind of the public. . . . As is evident from the present study, Mr. White proposes to give a frank portrait of a man as he sees him. He argues neither for or against his views or deeds. He aims solely to show the reader what manner of man this is that is playing so large a part in our public life. It is the sincere and unreserved expression of his own impressions, after having studied the man without bias or preconceit, that makes the value of the paper.[39]

In several White was certainly unreserved in his expression, particularly in the one about Platt, but editorial disclaimer aside he began most sketches from a "bias or preconceit," though he usually tried to be objective in his presentation, and sometimes succeeded. During most of the progressive era he was a free-lance publicist for Teddy Roosevelt; his article about William Howard Taft written for the *American Magazine* in 1908 provides an example of that. He wrote it to help boost Taft for the presidency; in fact, in the introduction to this collection he recalls conferring with Roosevelt about that sketch over lunch at the White House where TR told him, "don't hold the knife edge of your balance so perfectly poised in this piece that your readers won't see your bias" (vii). With our knowledge of later events it is no surprise to find that he rewrote the section about Taft thoroughly so his later readers would indeed not see his bias.

But on the whole he did not give revised definitive judgments about the figures chosen for this book, and David Hinshaw is wrong when he asserts, "There he gave final verdicts on most of them. Other writers have only filled out the details." Sometimes White did soften incidentals to conform to his later liberal stance, but he did that through minor changes in wording without seriously affecting his original judgments of principal figures. For example, in his 1902 portrait of Cleveland he referred to the 1894 Pullman Strike thus: "There came a time when the rabid discontent of the people broke out in riot. The great Chicago strike in the Mississippi Valley clutched business by the throat. In Illinois the governor of the State was clearly in sympathy with blatant anarchy. Then Grover Cleveland rose again as the despot of law and order, and with the arms of the Government of the United States quelled the mob."[40] In the book version he changed that passage to read:

There came a time when discontent broke out in riot. A great railroad strike centering at Chicago clutched business by the throat in the Mississippi Valley. In Illinois Governor Altgeld, a Populist Democrat, was clearly in sympathy with the strikers. He claimed they were about to win the strike. Altgeld's opponents feared that the striker's victory would be a surrender to anarchy. Altgeld held that the strikers had a just cause. His foes declared the mob should be quelled before the merits of the strike could be discussed. Then Grover Cleveland rose again as a despot of law and order, and with the arms of the Government of the United States quelled the mob, and of course broke the strike. (138)

But such instances of updating in the seven intact articles are infrequent.

Indeed, what is unusual is how well the implicit bias of his early and later views compare, because in the interval he became an ardent progressive and advocated many political reforms. But no matter how ardent an idealist he became, he was never blindly visionary about the game of politics. For he was a practiced player who understood and admired those who played well, even if they stretched the rules a bit. In the *Autobiography* he cites one of his experiences as a precinct committeeman in Emporia to give an example of local politics during a hot interparty contest. In the mandatory caucus held in his

ward he controlled the choice of delegates to the county convention
by recognizing only the names of his fellows in a prearranged, memo-
rized numerical order. One of the subalterns of Cy Leland happened
to attend and remarked to White afterward, at least as he remembered it, "Well, you fooled me. I thought you was one of them long-
haired, literary fellows. God! You pretty nearly got away with murder" (321). White knew politics, and that knowledge gave authority
to his magazine sketches.

Though he represented a rural point of view to his audience, he
was no hick. He understood from the first the *raison d'etre* of the late
nineteenth-century big-city boss, that in the potential chaos of tene-
ment districts overflowing from a constant stream of uneducated im-
migrants a feudal order is preferable to no order, the paternalism of a
political machine better than neglect. In his 1901 analysis of Richard
Croker he wrote: "A cautious rascal is safer than a vain demagogue.
A corrupt king is rather to be chosen than the anarchy of a million
hungry, shifty despots. Croker and his kind have their place in the
scheme of things."[41] He only expounded upon that thesis in his 1926
sketch of Al Smith where he acknowledged the rising importance of
urban America in determining national politics and wrote, "Crokerism
waned with the coming of a new century. Croker passed. A new order
appeared. All the politics that Al Smith learned of the old order
under Tom Foley, the local leader, was a capacity for teamwork, a
habit of industry, and the precious moral precept that it does not
pay to lie. Much may be said for the Croker kind of politics. It did
make square men who according to the morals of their day played a
fair, brave game, even when it was dirty."[42]

Another remarkable consistency about these sketches is in White's
purpose and technique. His purpose, as announced by *McClure's*, was
to show "what manner" of men these are who are playing so large
a role on the public stage. Thus his emphasis was upon his impression
of a man's moral character in the context of public life. In the book,
to his first chapter, "Croker: The Rise of a Cave Man," part of his
article in the *McClure's* series, he added a paragraph to announce his
purpose as he saw it in 1928: "The object of this study is to collect
and set down certain data available about the man Croker; to find
his family, genus, and species; to ascertain what he feeds upon; what
his place is in the scheme of things; that is, what part he and his kind
play in the conservation of political and social energy that is slowly
forcing the inevitable triumph of 'reason and the will of God' " (4).

This statement of intent can serve all his biographical writings: his subject is a type to be set against the social backdrop of his time. In that respect his sketches roughly fit the eighteenth-century genre of the extended "character."

In his maturity White was no religious or racial bigot, as witnessed by his vigorous attack of the Ku Klux Klan, but he did believe firmly in Aryan superiority, especially that of an Anglo-Saxon and Celtic heritage, perhaps because it was his own. Yet as a meliorist he had faith just as firmly in the importance of environment in determining character. So as touchstones in all his sketches he used genealogy and background very heavily, though he did moderate his focus on genealogy in the rewritten articles and admitted in his late sketch of Al Smith that we do not always know a man by the company he keeps. Still, from first to last, he grounded his methodology upon a nearly unqualified Darwinism to achieve an appraisal of his subject's moral development and stance. In the first two sentences, omitted from the book, of his magazine sketch of Hanna he baldly acknowledged that method and its source: "Mr. Herbert Spencer holds that life is a series of relations, and that man and the other creatures of the earth are the reflections of their environment. Assuming the truth of Spencer's contention, it may be instructive to know something of Marcus Alonzo Hanna's habitat."[43]

In each sketch he conveys the dominant impression derived from his appraisal through a repeated set of metaphors or a prevailing image cluster. He does it so obviously in the early sketches that rather than making device subservient to purpose, he draws attention to the device itself. For when the connotations of the device are striking, its visibility contributes to the impact of the piece and sometimes creates more heat than light. As an example, in his sketch of Platt, White constantly alludes to him as an earthworm and to his ways as a clammy delving in the dirt of New York politics: "After the defeat of Blaine at the Minneapolis Convention in '92, Platt returned to his earth at Albany. There he had begun a great subterranean work under the institution of popular government by the State; he went back to finish it."[44] No wonder "Earthworm Platt" threatened a libel suit. In his early portrait of Croker, White compared him to a hell-diver, a bird that does "God's work in the mud, which is as honorable a station as the arbor is—even if to our finite eyes the arbor may seem more beautiful. So when a man rises full of power, and daubed as to plumage with the muck of the marsh, we must measure him by the oriole."[45]

Apparently, the "Croker Bird" objected to that image, for he gave no more interviews to journalists that year, according to his biographer, Theodore L. Stoddard. In his later sketches White continued the device of the dominant trope but made it more subliminal, an organizing technique, not didactic decoration. For example, he viewed Cal Coolidge as a Vermont Yankee translated to the White House or saw Al Smith as a personification of New York City thrusting itself onto the national stage or presented Big Bill Thompson in the guise of an affable playboy, "big-hearted, free-handed and dull-witted," using Chicago as a toy.

Another similarity in his magazine sketches is motif, for he admired and emphasized certain character qualities: masculinity, vigor, honesty, loyalty, and frankness.[46] His two major political heroes, Hanna and Roosevelt, were antithetical in many of their social views, but in White's eyes both epitomized the moral traits he upheld. Of course, the moral code he referred to is that of politics in which to be true means never lie to your friends or once you give your word, keep it. Though he personally opposed Cleveland's election in 1892, he praised the man for his blunt, massive integrity; though he supported McKinley in 1896 and 1900, he criticized him for his frigid, calculating personality. Clearly, White tried to be just, to present a balanced appraisal of his subject, for he offered critiques based on values that were above crass partisanship, though he was not above putting in an occasional Republican puff. For example, in his 1900 sketch of Bryan, whom he had denounced in 1896 as a demagogue, he admitted, "Now the truth of the matter is that Mr. Bryan is not a demagogue. He is absolutely honest, which a demagogue is not."[47] In his 1925 sketch of Woodrow Wilson, whom he supported at Paris in 1919 as the "spiritual ruler of Christendom," he adhered to the same set of judgmental values when he observed:

Wilson's emotional defects amounted to moral defects. And whatever failure came to his career at the end was moral failure, greedy vanity for the quality and caliber of his own mind. Too often in his career—at Princeton, at Trenton, at Washington—he had prided himself on his ability to separate himself, as a man, from his personal obligations; to follow what he regarded as a principle, irrespective of the cost. He was suspicious in his dearest friendships. He broke personally, time and again, with men to whom he owed moral obligations, when he thought these men were not loyal to his intellectual conclusions; which means bluntly that he could not get along with men who differed with him, however much he might owe to them in decent human gratitude. This quality, at the last, isolated him. This quality attracted sycophants; but in his great crisis, it repelled strong men. (385)

In his articles, then, White attempted objectivity; and when that was impossible, he freely acknowledged it. In a footnote to his revised article about TR he warned that because of their friendship he probably was not "fair in estimating his weaknesses." Nevertheless, that estimate could still be acerbic. Referring to Roosevelt's sponsorship of Taft, he remarked that TR "in his day was probably the largest private consumer of human gold bricks in the country.... But whether Roosevelt tolerated men who loved him, or loved men whom he came to tolerate, or was just fooled in their qualities, no one knows" (331). As a writer of magazine sketches White built his reputation on such "objective partisanship." For he was a journalist who made his point of view and values clear to all and therefore wrote with integrity. But what attracted many to him was he also wrote with sparkle.

The Old Order Changeth. Another view of White as a magazine contributor is available in his book *The Old Order Changeth* (1910), a collection of six articles about ongoing changes in the spirit and form of American government that the *American Magazine* published as a leading series during 1909–10.[48] To the book he added an introduction for perspective and a conclusion for prognosis, then used the articles as separate chapters virtually untouched and in the same progression as the series. They exhibit White's work as magazine publicist and commentator, for in them he describes the movement of progressive legislation in the states and extrapolates causes and effects. He wrote them as he was finishing *A Certain Rich Man*, just before his six-months tour of Europe, and presents the same message in them as he does in the novel, but in the devices of expository prose (see chapter 4). In them he proclaims that the altruistic spirit of American democracy, vibrantly alive during the Civil War era but nearly buried afterward by the selfish forces released by rapid industrialization, is again ascendant. Once again "brotherhood is abroad in the land" (3). And, paradoxically, once again war is the mechanism of release, for according to him it was the Spanish American War that allowed the spirit of sacrifice to overcome the spirit of commercialism. In that one observation he reveals the moral stridency coloring much of his work and so characteristic of the reforming stance of other Rooseveltian progressives.

In the articles White surveys recent democratic changes in American government at every level and offers fresh data about their extent gathered from letters he wrote to officials in every state. The foremost impression he conveys with his extensive use of data is an uncharacteristic solemnity. In most of his magazine contributions, including his fiction, he is morally earnest, of course, but he leavens that earnestness with a breeziness and humor missing here. Here his purpose is to instruct, not to entertain or, like a muckraker, to shock. As White catalogs the specifics of change, he compiles in essence a descriptive handbook to the more widely advocated political reforms of the progressive era: the secret ballot; the publication of party finances; the primary; the direct election of U.S. senators; the initiative, referendum, and recall; and the commission form of city government. He also enumerates such other reforms as uniform accounting practices for cities, working men's compensation laws, extension of civil service lists, income and inheritance taxes, railroad regulations, etc. He embeds his data in interpretive commentary, of course, and tempers both with a political philosophy based on meliorism and aspiration. For example, his sixth article proclaims its thesis with the title "The Schools the Mainspring of Democracy" (chapter 7), which he develops with a survey of curricular reforms providing manual training and vocational and physical education programs. He then explains new state pension systems designed to draw better trained and more male teachers into the profession. All of this he advocates in order to keep teenage boys of impoverished families in school, which is necessary, he believes, because American democracy will only be as strong as all its citizens are well educated. Thus he suggests that other states follow Ohio's example and pay needy parents the equivalent of a teenage boy's wages while the child is in school because "the pittance that the child can earn is so little compared to the need of the state for that child's judgment formed by a trained mind in making public sentiment when he is grown, that it is folly to haggle over the expense account" (192).

In his final article, "The Courts the Check of Democracy" (chapter 8), he does let slip his professional pose when he accuses the federal judiciary of purposely hindering reform legislation of the previous decade. He argues forcefully that the federal courts are the last stronghold of plutocracy and that their assumption of an injunctive check against recent social legislation is not sustained by the constitution or by legal history. The courts, he asserts, should reflect the will of the people but instead reflect the will of the powerful, an assertion he then documents with a list of all federal judges and their sponsors for appointment. The topic of judicial interference was especially timely, for in August 1910, during a speaking tour of the West, TR shocked conservatives by espousing popular recall of state court decisions that nullified reform legislation and by attacking vigorously the obstructive attitude of the federal courts. As a publicist, then, White kept abreast, sometimes even ahead, of moderate liberal opinion and was a masterful teacher in "school by magazine." Testifying to his educational success is the fact that in a textbook edition *The Old Order Changeth* was used in college political science courses for more than a decade because it summarized the policies of those who, with their creed "of simple justice between man and man known as righteousness," formed the center of the Progressive Movement.

Syndicated Reporter

White garnered much of his national attention writing for newspaper syndicates as an early-day interpretive political reporter who covered the national conventions of both parties from 1904 through 1940, plus the Progressive party conventions in 1912 and 1916. He reported the 1896 Republican convention in St. Louis for the *Kansas City World*, missed both in 1900, but covered the 1904 conventions for *Collier's* and the *Saturday Evening Post*. Then in 1908 George M. Adams contracted with White at $1,500 per convention and brought him nationwide renown as a syndicated newspaper reporter.[49] His portly figure and cherubic face became familiar totems to the delegates of both parties and his reports carried the authority of much experience. And White syndicated more than just reports of political conventions. During the 1912 campaign, for example, he wrote a syndicated weekly article for the *Chicago Tribune*, another "on the Kansas situation" for the *Kansas City Star*, and yet another for Will Irwin's "Bull Moose syndicate."[50] During World War I he wrote by-lined propaganda articles on behalf of both the Creel Committee on Public Information and the Red Cross. Released through the Wheeler syndicate, so he wrote proudly to U.S. Senator Charles Curtis, they "reached forty newspapers from Boston to San Diego, with a total circulation of over five million."[51] Later he contracted to cover such public events as the 1919 Paris Peace Conference and the 1933 International Economic Conference in London, wrote interpretive series from his various European travels, and as a publicist submitted political features or commentary to his syndicate from time to time and wrote releases for the AP wire.

From its founding in 1930 to his death he worked for the North American Newspaper Alliance (NANA), "the leading specialized news agency" in the United States, according to press historian Edwin Emory.[52] With the influential *Times* as its New York representative, it served a geographically diverse group of metropolitan papers with a combined circulation of ten million during the 1930s. From the beginning of his career, in fact, White free-lanced for syndicates; as early as 1890 while working on the *El Dorado Republican* he sold newspaper verse and an occasional minion feature to the American Press Association, one of the major ready-print distributors.[53] Later he wrote for the McClure's Newspaper Syndicate, the Adams News Service, the Wheeler Syndicate, and the Bell Syndicate, in that order, each in its day representing large strings of newspapers.

Like his magazine articles and *Gazette* editorials, White's syndicated newspaper reports are nearly inaccessible. In the nature of things news stories are transient—"yesterday's newspaper wraps today's garbage." But we do have available some examples of his convention reports in *Politics: The Citizen's Business* and to a lesser extent in *What It's All About.* The first contains his Bell Syndicate stories of the 1924 conventions virtually untouched, the other versions of his NANA reports of the 1936 conventions. The latter he intended as little more than a minor period piece, for he speaks of it in the preface as but a fleeting picture of the 1936 campaign "as it stood in mid-August," of interest perhaps "in a hundred years if it is exhumed ... for the man who is trying to tell what happened at the turn of the tide during the first part of the second third of the century" (vi). Since the tide by no means turned in 1936, it has even less interest for that man. But in the other, though describing it in the preface as an ephemeral, "glimpsing book," White tried to give weight to his observations by stressing a thesis implicit in his syndicated copy, that the American political process had been changed by well-organized special-interest groups operating upon and within yet

outside the two-party system and that in order to understand the
mechanisms of American democracy we must recognize the forms
and power of those groups. As he explained in the preface,

when the convention stories were written, it was obvious that they contained oblique reference to what might be called the infection of the
party conventions by social and political units formed for the purpose of
making the citizen's private sentiment, public opinion. And it seemed to
the writer that these glancing references were sufficiently numerous and
sufficiently lucid to be set down in the pages of a book, so that real
students of politics and sociology might be attracted to this branch of
their subject. (vi)

Politics: The Citizen's Business.   *Politics: The Citizen's Business* consists of twenty chapters and a long appendix of convention
realia—platforms and sundry speeches. The first two and the last chapters were written as framework for the news reports, each making up
a short chapter: five for the perfunctory Republican convention,
which nominated Coolidge in a foregone conclusion; eleven for the
boisterous Democratic, that settled on John W. Davis after a long
fight. Then he added a longer chapter giving an early overview of
the election which he wrote originally for *Collier's*.[54] In chapters 1 and
2 White discusses eighteenth-century American constitutional theory
and history, then traces the formation of the two-party system in the
nineteenth century, which after the Civil War gave ascendancy to
plutocracy. He now sees the American political process influenced by
more diverse special interest groups, which he categorizes for extended analysis. Once again, he suggests, as intended by the framers
of the constitution, all citizens can have a voice in their government
by the new expedient of joining one or more of these special interest
groups: "The Constitution which our Fathers devised so wisely seems
to be made to hand for the purpose of the invisible governments that
of necessity have sprung up in a complicated civilization" (15). But
because these pressure groups function outside party bounds and
without constitutional checks, he calls for public disclosure laws to
regulate them so that "the invisible government become visible" (18).
Yet because of them, he believes, each citizen now has the opportunity to participate meaningfully in politics; he thus offers a "handbook" to the recent conventions.

   In the following chapters White changed his syndicated reports
slightly, putting them in the past tense and giving a few of his com-

ments the benefit of immediate hindsight, but otherwise they are as originally written. In covering the Republicans he wrote his usual Sunday preconvention piece, giving an old wheel horse's view of the issues and personalities involved as the delegates gathered in Cleveland to nominate Coolidge. But Coolidge walked to a nomination on a first ballot, with neither the Old Guard or remnants of the Progressives capable of bushwacking him. Thus, in his valedictory report White observed with disgust: "The lack of the fighting spirit which departed from the party when Roosevelt left it was reflected in this eventless convention. It was heavy with monotony" (40). The 1924 Democratic convention in New York City was not short or lacking in fighting spirit; it dragged on for sixteen days deadlocked on William McAdoo and Al Smith before finally compromising on Davis. And White's reports of it are vigorous because, unlike the Republican convention, it mirrored the social and emotional issues of the early 1920s.

In his reports White transcended the immediacy of politics to place issues or personalities in a larger, often quirky or humorous context. His coverage itself was not monotonous because he filed more than run-of-the-mill news reports. First of all, his copy was sprightly, good for a grin if not a laugh. Second, he selected events to support bylined commentary written from a much-experienced insider's point of view. That commentary was relatively impartial too—topical, lightly sketched political observations rather than partisan diatribes. Nineteen years earlier, in a short story he wrote about a young reporter on a country newspaper, White fingered the key to his own success: "the reporter who can go and bring back the soul of a meeting, the real truth about it—what the inside fights meant that lay under the parliamentary politeness of the occasion, who can see the wires that reach back of the speakers, and see the man who is moving those wires and can know why he is moving them; who can translate the tall talking into history he is a real reporter."[55]

What It's All About. White as syndicated reporter was a seasoned, astute, even iconoclastic observer, when his personal loyalties were not involved. But they were involved in *What It's All About*, a painfully ambivalent little book which he published in 1936 to support Alf Landon, one of his Kansas "boys," and at the same time disavow any connection with Landon's reactionary campaign organization. He was ambivalent for the same reason he had for years seemed politically schizophrenic on the national level—the peculiar nature of Kansas politics. In chapter 4 he explains that in his state "party lines are loosely drawn. Factional lines are tighter. It has been forty years since Kansas has elected on her state ticket below the office of governor anything but Republican candidates. Yet, in that time the state has had several Democratic senators, half a score of Democratic congressmen and three Democratic governors. But every biennium sees a healthy fight inside the Republican Party between the liberal and conservative factions..." (49–50). White as one of the bosses of his state's Republican liberal faction was in truth a captive generic liberal.

Like the 1924 handbook, *What It's All About* is part text, part appendix. Chapter 1 is from the *New York Times Magazine*; chapter 4 from a *Saturday Evening Post* sketch.[56] Chapters 2 and 3 condense his syndicated newspaper articles to give an insider's account of how the Republicans meeting again in Cleveland nominated Landon and put together a motley platform; chapters 5–7 are slightly rewritten versions of three of his reports about the Democratic convention in Philadelphia. In them he analyzes the Democrats as a new party, "in essence and politically, the creature of Hamilton." Though the book was ostensibly an apologia for Landon, White revealed in these accounts his reluctant admiration for FDR—for his frank facing of the issues with optimistic innovation, for his charismatic leadership as reflected in his brilliant acceptance speech: "It was ... a most amazing performance in setting, in words and the man—the man, the subject and the occasion. It was true oratory in a new day and time" (90). Headed by Pilate's weary question "What Is Truth?" the seventh and last chapter White wrote specifically for the book. In it he concludes, "This campaign is but an extension of the mid-summer madness at Cleveland and Philadelphia. Yet if at the end we keep our feet, if at the end we walk in reason and in common sense avoiding temptations to emotion and hysteria, the result, whatever it shall be, will be worth its cost" (100). That statement is not a ringing endorsement of Alf Landon, but it does testify to White's dilemma as a syndicated reporter interpreting the welter of national politics for millions of readers while trying to keep his feet within the Kansas Republican party and still "walk in reason and in common sense."

Chapter Four

A Victorian Sentimentalist: Fiction

When White was in his thirties and forties he was known nationally as an author of popular regional fiction, who was as much a spokesman for small-town America in that medium as in journalistic commentary. During those two middle decades of his life he published eight books of fiction, his total output, in the form of five collections of short stories (*The Real Issue, The Court of Boyville, Stratagems and Spoils, In Our Town,* and *God's Puppets*), two novels (*A Certain Rich Man* and *In the Heart of a Fool*), and one novelized travel tale (*The Martial Adventures of Henry and Me*). Of his fifty collected short stories the first fifteen appeared originally in limited circulation Kansas newspapers, the other thirty-five in the nationally known *McClure's Magazine, Saturday Evening Post, Scribner's Magazine,* or *Collier's Weekly.* His first novel was an immediate best-seller with some critics hailing it as "the fulfillment of a long-standing promise for a great American novel."[1] But his much-rewritten second novel fell far short of such a promise, receiving many negative reviews and selling poorly. After it he published only one in a projected series of short stories and within a few years his reputation as a writer of fiction had faded. Now he is regarded as a tertiary figure in American literature, a local-color realist of sentimental and melodramatic hue.

Though White may be so categorized and dismissed by literary historians, his fiction itself cannot be so lightly considered because it is symptomatic of his time and place. Some of his stories are simply magazine kitsch, but many transcend that category to stand forth as interesting regional fiction on subjects somewhat out of the ordinary. That includes his two novels too: though trite in theme and clumsy in structure, in them are the history and attitudes of an era. As the social historian Richard Hofstadter once pointed out, "what fails as literature is frequently significant as self-revelation or as a social document."[2]

White set many of his stories in Kansas during the Gilded Age; he traces in them the development of that region from the Civil War on and the changes in certain of its inhabitants. He wrote out of his own experiences, exploring the milieu he grew up in and the quintessential moral issue consuming his generation, the dichotomy between business values and human values. That dichotomy was a standard thematic source for hundreds of social problem stories during the progressive era, but White drew his from that source with an authority and an artless poignancy that especially appealed to his age. While his settings and characters were provincial, even personal, his attitudes were general American, a confused jumbling of the Epworth League with the GAR, the Social Gospel with the Gospel of Wealth, Emersonian idealism with Mark Hanna cynicism, Jeffersonian independence with Hamiltonian authority. The result of such a muddle was that White approached the problems of America's industrial revolution emotionally rather than analytically, relying on sentiment rather than intellect. He was content to reform a character instead of the system. His dependence on sentimentality in his stories led, of course, to didacticism, to contrived appeals to the heart, bringing about unlikely character changes and melodramatic endings. Though such sentimentalism destroyed his stories as "art," that is, as controlled exercises in the rhetoric of fiction, it did make them representative examples of American popular culture. Thus the critic Charles C. Baldwin claimed, "they teach and preach with gusto, with energy, with an optimism that is truly winning and wholly American. . . . American—that is what they are. And make no mistake—the best of Mr. White is the best of America. Not the best of which certain rarely gifted individuals are capable, but the best of the common man, the genius of the common man, his more generous impulses and his better judgment."[3]

In a review for *Collier's* of Sinclair Lewis's *Main Street*, White acknowledged it a notable achievement, a "powerful array of country-town facts . . . that all Americans should read—to take the conceit out of them," but it did not present the whole picture, he protested: "To fail to see the sheer power of sentiment in American life merely because you dislike sentimentality is bad art. Damn sentimentality if you will; but don't deny its presence and power in American life."[4] White did not deny the sordid in life, many of his stories testify to that, but he did not subscribe to the spirit of satire or the philosophy of deterministic realism that governed Lewis's selection of facts. For

White was a nondoctrinaire Christian, not an iconoclastic agnostic—a transcendentalist, not a materialist. In his fiction he reminds us that R. W. Emerson as much as J. D. Rockefeller contributed to the American dream. In 1920, at the start of a decade of postwar cynicism, Lewis viewed the life of wistful Carol Kennicott trapped in Gopher Prairie, Minnesota, as typical of many in small-town Main-Street America. And it was, but not of all. In 1896, the high-water year for Populist aspiration, Charles M. Sheldon, a Congregationalist minister from Topeka, Kansas, published *In His Steps*, a novel that explicated "muscular Christianity" to Middle America. It sold in the millions during White's lifetime, and many of its readers did try falteringly but earnestly to follow in Christ's steps. They lived on the same street as Carol Kennicott, but on the sunnier side. Lewis chose not to focus his camera on that side; Sheldon and White did.

The Real Issue

When a teenager in El Dorado, White read a review copy of Ed Howe's novel *The Story of a Country Town*; until then, he once told an interviewer, he "had read only the false and saccharine novels of the period which dealt not even remotely with life as he knew it."[5] Howe's realistic yet melodramatic treatment of suppressed passions in everyday rural life showed White that fiction could be about common people and local matters. Later, when he began to write newspaper fiction, he followed Howe's example and chose to write about life as he knew it. But he knew it different from Howe, the deeply pessimistic "Sage of Potato Hill." Although most of the fifteen stories in White's first collection, *The Real Issue: A Book of Kansas Stories* (1896), are realistic in subject, sentiment motivates the characters, didacticism governs the tone, and optimism sweetens the denouement. In his *Autobiography* White remembered those stories as "tear jerkers most of them, though some were just ebullient Kansas spirits" (287). But sentimental local color was not his exclusive affective principle here, for at least several are vague formula fiction with no Kansas connections. Still, a reviewer for *The Dial*, at that time a Chicago-based fortnightly, noticed publication of *The Real Issue* by reporting it contained "truthful stories of Kansas life, with occasional touches of humor and a heavy burden of pathos."[6]

"Bathos" would be a more accurate description of the earliest tale of that volume, "The Regeneration of Colonel Hucks." As White

told it, Hucks was a Civil War veteran who in 1890 had deserted the
GOP for the Alliance ticket against his wife's wishes but returned
tearfully two years later as a delegate to the state Republican convention at Topeka. When he got home his wife greeted him with "the
old regimental flag waving over the door. Inside of the house, he
observed that 'Mother' had brought out the pictures of Grant and
Sherman and Lincoln, which she had put away the year before." In
the center of that group was hanging their little dead son's faded-
blue soldier-cap she had sewn for the child just after the war. Though
shamelessly maudlin, the story did announce a theme that for some
reason White explored over and over again in his fiction, the welcomed return of the prodigal.[7] The other story about Hucks in that
collection, "The Homecoming of Colonel Hucks," is an equally sentimental, but this time also humorous, version of that theme. In it
Hucks and his wife revisit their old home in Ohio for the first time
after thirty years of homesteading and rearing a family in Kansas. But
they find their youthful, gay remembrances of Ohio, by which they
had always judged things in Kansas, to be grossly exaggerated, so they
return to Kansas early singing its praises all the way. It is a delight-
ful, homely little story and was one of two from this collection that
Sam McClure reprinted in his magazine.[8]

Another pair, "The Prodigal Daughter" and "The Record on the
Blotter," trace a variation on the same theme in the story of the
widower John Beasly, an inarticulate mechanic, and his beloved elder
daughter, Allie. Unguided by a mother, she becomes "fast" and eventually leaves home with a troupe of actors. When she returns humbled,
her father welcomes her with unwitting love and joy. But the cruelty
of gossiping, self-righteous neighbors causes her suicide, and her
father, in a flash of insight, hides her "shame" by falsely confessing
to her murder. The only other paired stories among the fifteen, "The
Chief Clerk's Christmas" and "The Story of a Grave," are slight
formula fiction concerning Chief Clerk Hawkins—a busy, "firm, taciturn, self-contained, repellent" businessman—a type whose only local
association is that he grew up near the town of Willow Creek, where
White set some of his later fiction. Hawkins eventually repents his
gruff, insensitive approach to life while dying at the grave of his
ex-wife's lover, who fortuitously had died at the same indefinite Far
West health spa to which Hawkins was sent.

Of the nine single stories five are just as slight, though one of
those, "That's for Remembrance," the critic and author Brander Mat-

thews thought well enough of to plagiarize the plot several years later.[9] It is a five-finger exercise in pathos in which a man fulfills a promise to his dead first wife when he gives his second wife, on her wedding night, a letter of transfer from the first. And another, "The Reading of the Riddle," is an awkward tale that has an ironic appeal because it anticipates the mood of Sherwood Anderson's *Winesburg, Ohio*— a book which White condemned as from "a maggoty mind."[10] The story is about Flora McCray, a wallflower who has a strange psychosexual epiphany during a night buggy ride home from a taffy-pull. However, four of the singles are of somewhat larger significance. Two of them, "The Story of Aqua Pura" and "A Story of the Highlands," are restrained, realistic tales about the boom that lured settlers to the arid plains of western Kansas during the atypically lush years of the early 1880s and then collapsed in the drought of the following years to destroy their hopes and lives. Both stories are memorable bits of local color.

The title story, "The Real Issue," is of interest because it introduces a subject, Gilded Age politics, and a character, Kansas Congressman Tom Wharton, that White developed later in the stories of *Stratagems and Spoils.* In this story, remembering his earlier idealism and fatigued by five terms of back-room deals in the House of Representatives, Wharton tells his hometown friend and campaign manager, Ike Russell, that he has decided not to run again. Several days later, unable to relinquish his place in the game, he once more deals through Russell for reelection. The subject of the fourth story, "The King of Boyville," comes from White's remembrance of his El Dorado boyhood. The story concerns us because Sam McClure enjoyed it, paid to reprint it, and recruited White to write more like it. The "King" is Winfield "Piggy" Pennington, a young village tough so painfully shy around girls he cannot speak to his Heart's Desire. For relief he terrorizes other boys his age or younger but eventually speaks to her with flowers, and for him a new era dawns.[11]

Half the stories in this "Book of Kansas Stories" have no specific locale and none is truly memorable. Yet the book was a moderate success, receiving generally favorable reviews in many Midwestern newspapers and in several national journals and selling well, though Way and William's bankruptcy in 1899 impeded later sales. How much of that success was due to perceived merits is hard to say. For White promoted the book unabashedly and some reviewed it because of its serendipity with "What's the Matter with Kansas?" The well-known critic and editor Robert Bridges, for example, writing under the pseudonym "Droch," connected them in his generous review in the humor magazine *Life* to conclude with a quotation from the editorial: "Kansas may contain the 'most picturesque lot of cranks on God's green earth'—but there is one among them who can write a short story when he isn't sloshing around among the populists. So here's a hand to William Allen White, of the Emporia *Gazette*."[12] That applause gave White quite an ego-boost. In the *Autobiography* he recalled how he reacted to that review: "It was a moment in life never to be forgotten.... The printer, the reporter, the editorial writer on the *Star*, the country editor wrestling three days a week with his pay roll, with his petty cares and troubles—all these skins which I had worn were cast aside. I was a young author" (288).

The Court of Boyville

White's next book, *The Court of Boyville*, consists of the six stories he wrote for *McClure's* as a spin-off from the Boyville story in *The Real Issue*. Doubleday & McClure Co. published it with a prologue and four poems in October 1899 in time for the Christmas trade, binding it handsomely and illustrating it with artwork accompanying the previous magazine appearances. The firm projected a first printing of 6,000 copies and seem to have judged the initial market well, for sales totaled nearly 5,000 by the first of the year, but later "editions" moved much more slowly. Many newspapers noticed it favorably in their book review columns but no major journal reviewed it. Given White's spreading reputation among newspaper editors and the peculiar nature of the book, that is not surprising because many viewed it as juvenile literature, though White clearly wrote it for adults. Thus librarians placed the book among their children's collections, and a Kansas school superintendent publicly urged that the book be suppressed because it glorified the wrong values for children.[13]

In these tales of rough-hewn boyhood White added Bud Perkins to his earlier cast of Piggy Pennington, Mealy Jones, Abe Carpenter, Jimmie Sears, and Heart's Desire and set them specifically in the frontier village of Willow Creek, Kansas. In the prologue, though, he claimed universality for the collection because boyhood is a timeless state of mind—"Boyhood was old when Ninevah was a frontier post." It has its own moral code, chooses "its own sovereign, makes

its own idols." Insofar as that code came into conflict with the adult
world in these stories, they had the same appeal as the popular practical joke humor of *Peck's Bad Boy and His Pa.* But White's vein
of humor was much more sentimental than George W. Peck's, for
he stressed nostalgia more than confrontation and aimed at giving
his readers a lump in the throat instead of a stitch in the side.

Two stanzas from the introductory poem "A Wail in B Minor"
provide us the tone of the volume:

> Where now is the small boy who spat on his bait,
>   And proudly stood near the foot of the class,
>   And always went "barefooted" early and late,
> And washed his feet nights on the dew of the grass?
>
> Oh where and oh where is the old-fashioned boy?
>   Has the old-fashioned boy with his old-fashioned ways,
> Been crowded aside by the Lord Fauntleroy—
>   The cheap tinselled make-believe, full of alloy
>   Without the pure gold of the rollicking joy
> Of the old-fashioned boy in the old-fashioned days?   (2)

Later, though, in *Boys Then and Now* (1926), originally an article
in the *American Magazine* that Macmillan issued as a slender book,
White recognized that his remembrance of the "old-fashioned boy"
had a Peter Pan quality to it.[14] For he argued that Kansas in its early
days was a tough place for children, and as the frontier village of the
1870s developed into the civilized town of the 1920s its children were
better cared for, made better use of their leisure, and were better
educated. But he still looked back on the days of his boyhood with
nostalgia.

The first tale of the collection, "The Martyrdom of Mealy Jones,"
traces an evil day in the life of goody-good Harold Jones, contemptu-
ously dubbed "Mealy" by his fellows, who persuade him to go down
to the swimming hole against his mother's standing injunction. There
he petulantly gets in a fight with the new boy, Bud Perkins, who has
tied Mealy's fancy shirt in knots, then soaked it in the creek, and
discovers that by the code of Boyville one must fight alone. He is
"saved" by his father who to his shame canes him begging and hop-
ping before the other boys, then marches him home to Mother, whose
sympathies he enlists to Father's discomfort. But that night father

and son make up with a mutual sob. Especially do we have sobs in "A Recent Confederate Victory," a maudlin tale about Bud Perkins whose father, a "no-'count" Confederate veteran, drifts into town only to die and leave Bud a charge upon the county. After much pathos, and some insight into a child's inarticulate grief, the story concludes with "little Miss Morgan," a middle-aged spinster who had just finished rearing the last of her brother's orphans, literally lifting Bud from off his father's grave and giving him a home.

Fortunately, the other four stories are not as cloyingly sentimental. "While the Evil Days Come Not" is about Piggy Pennington's "tragic" misunderstanding with his Heart's Desire whom he fears favors Mealy Jones; she does not. "James Sears: A Naughty Person" details Jimmie's moody reactions to the birth of another sister, which he grudgingly accepts after his mother demonstrates understanding of his jealousy. "Much Pomp and Several Circumstances" is the most clearly comic story of the book. Brother Baker catches Bud Perkins, the South End Champ, disturbing church services by jabbing a North Ender with a pin, so Miss Morgan refuses Bud permission to go to a much-anticipated circus. After prolonged agony he persuades her to let him go where, unfortunately, he and his buddies get into a running battle with the North End boys to their mutual destruction. Bud limps home to certain disgrace. But soon after his sneaking through the kitchen door, a North End mother marches up to the front porch with disheveled son in tow to demand that Miss Morgan produce Bud and punish him. He makes his own even more bedraggled appearance, pleads self-defense, and enlists her sympathetic support.

The last sketch, "The Herb Called Heart's Ease," is a short postscript in which Piggy Pennington in the velvet of an evening communes with nature, which brings intimations of immortality to that dirty-footed, clean-souled boy. Perhaps that is why Mark Van Doren gave such a favorable assessment to the book in *Contemporary American Novelists 1900–1920*: White "understands the pathos of boyhood, seen not so much, however, through the serious eyes of boys themselves as through the eyes of reminiscent men reflecting upon young joys and griefs that will shortly be left behind and upon little pomps that can never come to anything. *The Court of Boyville* is now hilariously comic, now tenderly elegiac. None of Mr. White's contemporaries has quite his power to shift from bursts of laughter to sudden, agreeable tears."[15] Many of us, though, do not find a sudden shift to tears so agreeable.

Stratagems and Spoils

In 1898 Robert Bridges, editor of *Scribner's* who as a free-lancer had favorably reviewed *The Real Issue*, asked White to write for that dignified literary monthly. White agreed and in June 1899, before he had finished his Boyville stories for *McClure's, Scribner's* printed the first of four long, serious tales that White wrote for it over the next two years about Missouri Valley politics. The *Saturday Evening Post* printed a fifth story, during September and October 1901, on the same general subject, then the Scribner firm published those five stories together with illustrations and a brief preface as the book *Stratagems and Spoils* (1901). White tied the plots of the stories together casually either by a repeated appearance of characters or with the mutual setting of Pleasant Ridge, Kansas. And he connected them thematically by exploring versions of a similar subject, a woman's influence for good or bad upon American politics. Dedicated to the *Kansas City Star*, "an honest newspaper," the collection is earnestly didactic in the soon-to-be popular mode of muckraking political fiction.

In the preface White warns us, sententiously, that in the following stories he has rejected "the accepted motive of fiction," the sentimental love affair of a young man and woman, because it is but a prologue to the more serious interests of life. He has chosen instead, he tells us, to write of mature men and women whose passions affect the intertwined fields of business and politics, arenas in which greater human interests are at stake. He kept to that subject, the structure of Gilded Age politics, in four of his five later books of fiction. But in his novels and some of his later stories he forgot his other resolve and returned to young love as the principal motive, to the disgust of H. L. Mencken, who complained that in *A Certain Rich Man* White insisted that "the impulse which leads a young man of, say twenty-four years, to seek marriage with some particular young woman of, say twenty two, is by overwhelming odds the most elevating, valuable, noble, honorable and godlike impulse native to the human consciousness."[16] In returning to the sexual impulse etherealized, White was but true to his own deeply sentimental nature. When he turned in the 1920s to the writing of biography rather than fiction it was due not only to grief for his daughter but also because he was middle-aged and not so vulnerable to certain sentiments. As he explained much later to the critic Robert Van Gelder: "'Fiction is a matter of glands.' When one is no longer personally interested in sex and when anger has been succeeded by mellowness, then it is time to quit writing fiction."[17]

In a long, favorable notice of *Stratagems and Spoils* in the *North American Review*, W. D. Howells especially liked the first story of the collection, "The Man on Horseback," because it "is at every moment honest."[18] Joab T. Barton, president of the Corn Belt Railroad System and a powerful financier who controls politics in his part of the Missouri Valley, expects easy renewal of his city street railway franchise. But the local Civic Federation opposes him and enlists the casual aid of George, his playboy only child, whose otherwise most recent interest was young Mrs. Kelsey, second wife of Jim, a powerful political boss and one of Joab's creatures. Joab's wife, the dictator of local society, knows Mrs. Kelsey is using George to social climb, hates her accordingly, and resolves never to recognize her. George dies. Joab and wife grieve; their struggles seem in vain. But Jim's threat not to support renewal of the "all-important" railway franchise causes Joab to swallow his grief and roughly force his prostrated wife to accept publicly the condolences of Mrs. Kelsey as her price for guaranteeing Jim's loyalty.

The next story, "A Victory of the People," also features the crucial political influence of a married woman, but for good, not harm. Because of the death of an incumbent U.S. senator, well-meaning but machine-backed Governor Charles Rhodes must appoint someone to finish the term. These are the days before direct election, and this appointment is important to the power balance within the state party in that the two leading candidates are Tom Wharton, warhorse of the Old Guard, and John Gardiner, hero of the "anti-gang" faction. Suave Harvey Bolton, close friend of Rhodes and general counsel for the Corn Belt Railroad, under pressure from the company persuades the governor to appoint Wharton, though Rhodes wants instead to appoint Bolton because Wharton's reputation will not wash. But Bolton refuses to give up his lucrative law practice to become a political errand boy. When Mrs. Rhodes, a charismatic middle-aged woman, discovers Bolton has softened her husband's dilemma with the promise of a large contribution to his next campaign, she rejects it as a bribe, confronts Bolton, successfully appeals to his sense of humor, and he lets the governor announce John Gardiner's appointment, to the surprise of all.

Two stories, "A Triumph's Evidence" and "The Mercy of Death," are both overwritten melodrama. The first records the courtship by Henry Myton of Julia Fairbanks, the pretty Eastern-educated daughter of Judge Fairbanks of Pleasant Ridge. Henry had returned to town to pick up his law practice after losing his party's nomination for a third term as a U.S. congressman because of his heretical vote against its money plank. On psychic rebound he notices Julia and announces his interest: "The moan of the prairie surf rose like a distant diapason. Myton started from his chair impulsively. The spell upon his tongue was loosened for a moment, and he spoke all the poetry that was throbbing in his soul" (102–3). Taking Julia's professed idealism at face value, he seeks to please her by turning from halfhearted political independence to fervid idealism as he rises above party considerations to finish out his term a reformer. But she fails them both later when the state legislature deadlocks in naming a U.S. senator. Seduced by a chance at the cultural fleshpots of Washington, she persuades Myton to sell out to Joab Barton and become another kept man in the Senate.

"The Mercy of Death" details the final days of U.S. Senator Tom Wharton, who by trading on his office had amassed a fortune of several millions. But he overreached himself by speculating on the Chicago commodity market, was wiped out, and tries to recover by forcing Ike Russell, at that time his state's treasurer, to "lend" him $75,000 in school bonds to use as collateral. He again loses and, drinking heavily, crudely blackmails a District of Columbia utility company for $50,000 by threatening to push a bill favoring its competitor. This time his tactics are documented by Senator Felt—his political, cultural, and moral nemesis—who he learns plans to expose his criminality on the floor of the Senate. Desperate, Wharton sends a message to his mistress, in whose house he had temporarily stashed the school bonds, to deliver them so he can redeem the utility company's transfer of funds to his bank account and thereby deny Felt's attack, only to find she has taken the bonds and run. That night, while despairingly playing poker with his cronies, "fear twisted his nerves tighter and tighter . . . suddenly he tossed a card into the air, then threw his face upward, with an indescribable look of resentful anger upon his features. But his eyes were wild and staring, and his head dropped to the table with a thump. When they wiped the froth from his mouth Tom Wharton was dead" (196).

The final story, "A Most Lamentable Comedy," published in the *Saturday Evening Post* in 1901, is also of interest for White's sharply

satiric portrayal of Populism, which Howells criticized in his review
as "pitilessly hard." It confirms that the sardonic conservatism White
evinced in "What's the Matter with Kansas?" was much more than
skin-deep, that it was an attitude he did not miraculously slough off
upon meeting TR. In the story Dan Gregg, a ne'er-do-well street-
corner philosopher from Pleasant Ridge, gets himself nominated governor on the Populist ticket by exploiting popular unrest with hypnotic
oratory learned as a paid Alliance organizer. Fascinated by his performance, James McCord, liberal professor of political science at the
state university, and Mrs. Baring, middle-aged widow of established
independence and social prestige, accept his promise and become his
mentors. McCord takes him in hand, tones up his campaign and
person, and gets him elected. Mrs. Baring serves honorably as a
vivacious social ideal. Together they raise him above himself only to
discover that he has lost his footing. He poses as the White Knight
of Reform but unchivalrously keeps his wife, whom he now considers
insipid and tacky, at home in Pleasant Ridge. As his term progresses
Gregg, though personally honest, proves so incompetent an administrator that corruption flourishes in state institutions. Though Mc-
Cord protests, Gregg chooses to ignore state problems to stump the
nation for The Cause and Gregg. But to his surprise, the people
soundly repudiate the Populist ticket in the next election, and he
sordidly reverts back to type "with a laugh that sounded like a rip-
saw in a knot," his fantasy of power shattered.

"A Most Lamentable Comedy" is a conservative's snide extrapola-
tion of the career of such a man as Populist Congressman "Sockless
Jerry" Simpson of Kansas, a view White repented soon afterwards.[19]
But in it, and in the other stories of this volume, he also proclaimed
a view of social change he never repudiated, even in the potential
chaos of the 1930s, a Dickensian view, a "pietistic" view, that progress depends on personal, not legislated morality. For McCord observed
to Dick Turner, an aide to Gregg: "He forgets that the world moves
slowly. That the same people are here now that were here two and
four years ago, and voting a reform ticket doesn't make these people
perfect. You know, Dick, you can't help the world much by voting
your neighbor better. The way to help is to be better, more unselfish,
kinder, and broader-gauged yourself" (287). *Strategems and Spoils*,
then, consists of sermons on American politics with their lessons taken
from the popular doctrine of secular Christianity, which White sub-
scribed to throughout his life. Thus he was pleased to report in his

autobiography that Teddy Roosevelt, the most prominent American political exponent of that faith, declared for many years that book to be "the best picture of American politics he knew" (320).

In Our Town

Much less serious or pretentious, *In Our Town* (1906) brings together eighteen local-color short stories White wrote for the *Saturday Evening Post* plus one for *The Century*. They are light fictional vignettes of small-town characters as seen by the local newspaper editor, simple morality tales for the most part with the same blend of pathos and comedy Mark Van Doren found in the Boyville collection. White wrote two of the stories as a frame for the others. In the first, "Scribes and Pharisees," the narrator announces his rationale: "the country newspaper office is the social clearing-house" where the "editor and his reporters sooner or later pass upon everything that interests their town." In the last, entitled "Thirty," the journalist's sign off, he editorializes about the book's motif as he perceived it: "passing the office window every moment is someone with a story that should be told," for "if each man or woman could understand that every other human life is as full of sorrows, of joys, of base temptations, of heartaches and of remorse as his own, which he thinks so peculiarly isolated from the web of life, how much kinder, how much gentler he would be!" (363). Fortunately, such subsumed didacticism did not mar the majority of the tales, which are humorous, sensitive, detailed treatments of country-town life.

These seventeen sketches range the town's social strata from Red Martin, a drunken gambler, to John Markley, a lascivious old banker, from the slovenly typesetter "Princess" Swaney to deposed social lioness Priscilla Winthrop. A couple of the tales are temperance sermonettes ("And Yet a Fool" and "Sown in Our Weakness"), several are hackneyed pieces about character types ("The Coming of the Leisure Class" and " 'A Babbled of Green Fields"). But the rest are candid photos taken by a country editor, with the help of his staff, and portray a diversity of human attitudes against accurately delineated backgrounds. Only such a narrator would know that in "A Kansas Childe Roland," for instance, he should focus upon a local ruckus about moving the farmers' hitching racks out of the courthouse square to reveal the truth about the electoral defeat of corrupt state senator Ab Handy.

Anyone who has grown up in a small town and sat around a kitchen table listening to his parents and others connect community gossip to the genealogies of local families can testify to the authenticity of many of these stories. For example, in the preliminaries of "A Bundle of Myrrh" our narrator notes "the kinology of a country town is no simple proposition. After a man has spent ten years writing up weddings, births and deaths, attending old settlers' picnics, family reunions and golden weddings, he may run into a new line of kin that opens a whole avenue of hitherto unexplainable facts to him, showing why certain families line up in the ward primaries, and why certain others are fighting tooth and toe-nail" (120). The story that follows is about "Aunt" Martha Merryfield, a salty old widow who was one of eleven Perkins children related to the numerous Morton clan. The society editor, Miss Larrabee, turns to her as the town's kinology expert, but Aunt Martha cannot abide the paper's pretense that its town is a simple democracy with no cliques or crowds. Much of the tale, then, is our narrator's report of Aunt Martha's documentary about the town's class lines as delivered to the society editor. But it ends with a sentimental kicker. When the simple old bachelor and retired town clerk Jim Purdy dies, Miss Larrabee walks in on Aunt Martha racked by grief and discovers an unexpected relationship. Martha and Jim were lovers just before the Civil War. At its outbreak he joined the Union Army, ignorant that she was carrying his child. He was soon reported killed, and their baby died within a year. After the war Martha married Judge Merryfield; and after several years of confused wanderings Jim returned, a psychic casualty of Confederate prisons. Over the years Martha never flinched, living quietly with the judge, bearing his children but treasuring Jim in her heart. "No simple proposition" is country-town kinology.

Seven of the stories feature the newspaper's own staff. In them White incorporates details from Emporia and the *Gazette*, referring to the town's large Welsh community, using names of local people and places (Everett Fowler, Mike Wessner, Exchange Street, Lebo, "Possum Holler"), and interpolating several of his own editorials and journalistic antics. "The Casting Out of Jimmy Myers," for example, tells of a crackerjack young reporter who has a consistent run of bad luck. He writes a paid local on behalf of the town photographer criticizing an itinerant frame peddler, who turns into an irate, determined woman flourishing a rawhide whip. He writes up the funeral of the wife of a prominent citizen and his copy gets mixed with a

paid hardware item he turned in earlier: "Died—Mrs. William Gilsey.
Prepare for the hot weather, my good woman. There is only one
way now; get a gasoline stove, of Hurley & Co., and you need not
fear any future heat" (164). He prefaces a humorous story about an
erring husband with Kipling's lines "And this is the sorrowful story /
Told as the twilight fails, / While the monkeys are walking together, / Holding each other's tails!" only to have the printer trans-
pose a rule, placing that verse at the bottom of an announcement of
a wedding uniting two socially important local families (169). Dis-
mayed by such a jinx, the editor helps Jimmy obtain a job on another
paper, but just before he goes he suffers yet another contretemps.
Parson Frank Milligan, an irascible, self-advertising pest, overhears
Jimmy tell the new man in explicit detail to avoid the parson as a
plague, and Jimmy must take a last flying trip out the office back
door. White had himself suffered a version of each faux pas.

In "The Tremolo Stop" our editor tells of middle-aged tramp
printer Simon Mehronay who wandered into the office one day from
somewhere in Texas, picked up a composing stick, and became an
employee. Gradually he moved from the backshop to the editorial
side. Though he sometimes went on a binge, he was such an innocent and wrote whimsical copy with such ease and good humor that
he was beloved by all. One day the staff discovered his keeping
company with Columbia Merley, a starchy spinster who taught Hel-
lenic philosophy and Greek at the local college. Then they learned
that if he stayed sober three years she would marry him. He visibly
brightened at the prospect and for three years his "pieces" scintil-
lated and circulation increased. Then they married and she took him
to New York City where he found a better-paid slot and lives happy
and sober. Not an exciting plot perhaps, but it is of contextual interest because White used several of his own burlesque pieces and
sentimental editorials as examples of Mehronay's copy.[20] And, curiously, the story anticipates life insofar as it foreshadows Walt Mason's
later cure and career, for Mason decided while drying out at the
Keeley Institute in 1907 to apply for a job at the *Gazette* because
of the humor and kindness inherent in White's writings; in 1920
Mason retired to California, a sober and successful syndicated colum-
nist. Not so kind is "Our Loathed but Esteemed Contemporary,"
which features the editor's defeated rival, General A. Jackson "Bull"
Durham, proprietor of the *Statesman*; for it glances patronizingly at
White's own victory over former Lieutenant Governor C. V. Esk-

ridge of the *Emporia Republican*.[21] But whether or not we disregard that unkind reference, this story presents us with a vivid portrait in local colors of an old frontier editor as he and his days of unprincipled personal and political journalism fade away.

Because White was a well-established author by 1906, many of the literary journals of the "Eastern Establishment" favorably reviewed *In Our Town*. For instance, the reviewer in the *New York Times* "Saturday Review of Books" remarked, "It is late in the day to commend Mr. White as a graphic writer and a keen observer. His reputation is established all over the country. His present book is ... a cheerful book" that shows "the American people themselves just as they are in this very hour."[22] White was particularly pleased by the letter of praise from Mark Twain, himself an old newspaperman, who wrote him that he thought *In Our Town* a charming book. It still has charm: Walter Johnson, biographer of White, thinks that of all his fiction it "still makes enjoyable reading after the era that produced the book has passed away."[23]

A Certain Rich Man

In the novel *A Certain Rich Man* (1909) White presents a vivid cyclorama of Midwestern social history that transcends his didactic, clumsily contrived mode of narration to stand forth as his best work of fiction. He started it in 1905 and, with Sallie as an active partner, wrote it in three years during summers in Colorado and slack moments in Emporia, then during another year he cut it in half and rewrote it several times before turning the manuscript over to the Macmillan Company early in 1909. Though his plot traces the melodramatic rise and demise of John Barclay, Missouri Valley milling tycoon, White's real subject is the impact of the Gilded Age on the citizens of Sycamore Ridge, Kansas, as it grows from frontier village to twentieth-century town. Though his characters are types with transparently symbolic motives, they rise above caricature to embody a time, place, and action with a truthfulness rendered meaningful precisely because they are types. The authority with which he paints his cyclorama comes from an extensive use of intimate details from his childhood in El Dorado and early adulthood in Emporia, Lawrence, and Kansas City. Thus the reviewer for *The Outlook* remarked that the novel "is, above all, American in its spirit, its intimate knowledge of every-day American life, its dialogue, its fun and its pathos. ..."[24]

And a reviewer for the *New York Times* enthusiastically praised the novel for holding "the mirror up to more that is truly native and characteristic in American life than has been reflected by any other story teller who has essayed the task."[25]

The novel starts in 1857 with seven-year-old John Barclay interrupted in his play along Sycamore Creek to guide a band of Indians to the raw-new village of Sycamore Ridge, an adventure that once happened to Willie White. There we meet John's mother, Mary Barclay, widow of a New England abolitionist who had broken with his wealthy father to support the Cause in Kansas, only to be shot during a skirmish at Westport Landing on the Missouri border. Mary is an indomitable idealist who takes in washing to stay on at the village to pay tribute to her husband's spirit. But their son inherited much of the acquisitive Yankee nature of his paternal grandfather, so his life's story epitomizes a struggle between the forces of idealism and materialism, the American Zeitgeist. As White views it, that struggle triggered the Civil War which traumatized the nation for more than a generation. In Sycamore Ridge the war starts early, in 1860, with a clash between a group of slave-state border ruffians and free-state irregulars, who include the ex-horse thief Lige Bemis (later Judge Bemis, Barclay's unprincipled political henchman). Then in 1861 when the call goes out for Union volunteers, all of the men in the village ride away to war, including eleven-year-old John and his friend Bob Hendricks who stow away in a provisions wagon and witness the battle of Wilson's Creek. The bloody reality of battle horrifies John who is lamed for life there by a bullet in the foot. He spends the rest of his childhood back in Sycamore Ridge where his mother is now the school teacher.

John is only fifteen and still in school when the other veterans return home; among them are men who will be important figures in his epic: General Philomen Ward, lawyer and idealistic social reformer; General Madison Hendricks, pragmatic banker; Colonel Martin Culpepper, pollyanna land developer; Captain Watts McHurdie, diminutive harness maker and whimsical poet nationally renowned for one patriotic song; and Lieutenant Jake Dolan, livery stable owner, local politician, and soothsaying drunk. At that time John's life is that of Boyville growing up; however, busied by odd jobs, he already shows a hard, acquisitive spirit that is soothed only by his self-elevating love for Ellen Culpepper, whose sister Molly is the life-light for chum Bob Hendricks. The two boys are inseparable and attend the state university together, during which time Ellen dies, leaving John again wounded. After earning college degrees, Bob and John return home where Bob enters his father's bank and John sets up a law practice with General Ward.

The next decade of our story is full of local color straight out of White's own life, such as the armed county-seat war of 1873 between Sycamore Ridge and Minneola in which John helps save the court-house for his town (similarly "Old Doc" White fought for the court-house in El Dorado). John's prominent role in that year-long struggle taught him dirty politics and brought him legal business from the Corn Belt Railroad, a force which makes his later career possible be-cause railroads controlled the economy and government of Kansas and the Midwest for at least four decades, as White views events. Thus John Barclay eventually becomes the J. D. Rockefeller of the Plains, monopolizing wheat rather than oil by using Standard Oil's method of unethical shipping rebates. Less dramatic than a county seat fight but just as real for "mise en scene" is the rapid transforma-tion of Sycamore Ridge from self-sufficient rural village to industrially dependent town. Yet during that period of inordinate economic and social change, the slow pace of life and the attitudes of the citizenry alter slowly, as they are exhibited at Watts McHurdie's harness shop, where the principals of the story drop by to refight the battles of the war and mull over events of the day. And, through the scrim of John's personal life, as he progresses from careless bachelor to settled mar-ried man, White highlights the democratic ambience of nineteenth-century frontier-town sociability, which he got to know in the 1880s as a young man playing piano in a small band and calling off dances around Butler County. Several years after college, John was still a single among the members of Sycamore Ridge's "Spring Chicken Club," chumming around with Bob Hendricks and Molly Culpepper; he then becomes attached to Jane Mason of Minneola, whom he mar-ries and loves, though she is not his soulmate as was Ellen. As a husband he is exemplary; his marriage is happy, his tastes simple. But as a businessman he is evil incarnate.

During the mid-1870s, trading upon hard times, John floats the Golden Belt Wheat Company and uses deceptive purchase contracts to lease wheat lands from impoverished farmers of the area. Using his energies and persuasive powers, he prevents a run on the tottering Hendricks' bank and involves it and Colonel Culpepper in his scheme, sending Bob off to hustle Eastern financial circles for necessary support. With Bob out of the way John forces General Hendricks to forge notes to keep the bank and company solvent, but hard times persist and their efforts seem doomed. Then enters dapper, flighty Adrian Brownwell, the new editor of the *Sycamore Ridge Banner* (secretly a former deserter from the Confederate Army and possessor of a small tainted cache of gold eagles) who unknowingly saves their enfeebled bank with a crucial cash deposit. Brownwell then woos Molly Culpepper, with the unspoken encouragement of John and her father, who wish to keep him and thus his deposit in town. John forces Bob, who is ignorant about these matters, to remain in New York, and Molly sacrifices Bob to marry Brownwell out of weakness and loyalty to her father. Times have improved, the bank is back on its feet, and John takes over the farmers' lands for a song. But General Hendricks dies from shame and Bob comes home to discover heartbreak and swindle. He breaks with John, continues to cherish Molly, and gradually builds a national reputation from his home in Sycamore Ridge as a steadfast, practical, political reformer.

Barclay ruthlessly develops his business empire, aided by his patented "Economy Door Strip," a simple device used on all railroad grain cars to grant him preferential shipping rebates. But during John's rise our narrator also develops the stories of other local citizens not so heartlessly successful and judges them all by the parliament that drifts in and out of McHurdie's shop, to John's pronounced disadvantage. Through Lige Bemis and Gabriel Carnine, another reprobate, John callously buys politicians and influence at the state and federal level. He founds subsidiary companies, assembles a large milling trust, becomes president of the Corn Belt Railroad, then organizes all under the charter of the National Provisions Company, a huge holding firm seemingly impervious to law. Meanwhile, though his office center is in Chicago, he maintains his home in Sycamore Ridge where his one child, Jeanette, grows up watched over by Jane and Grandma Barclay, who disapproves of her son's hard materialism. One summer, home from the University of Kansas and alone with her grandmother while her parents are in Europe, Jeanette falls in love with Neal Ward, upstanding son of General Ward, a widely respected but now penniless social protester. Neal is a senior at the small local college, which bears his father's name. After Neal graduates, John takes him on for three years as his private secretary to teach and test him before allowing him to marry Jeanette, who greatly respects her father and his wishes. Formerly Barclay's law partner,

General Ward worries that John will seduce the boy with his obsessed drive for wealth and power at any moral cost. But the century has turned and times are changing; Barclay finds his empire under attack, his political credit diminishing.

Early in 1903 Congress prohibits railroad rebates, sets up a Department of Commerce and Labor, and gives its staff power to enforce federal laws against national companies. The infamous National Provisions Company is the first to be investigated, and John discovers that all of his purchased political power cannot stop the inquest. A plenipotentiary inspector appointed by the president takes a deposition from Neal because he knows many of the details of Barclay's collusions. Neal now faces his cardinal test of character: he can lie under oath, keep Jeanette, and ultimately inherit Barclay's wealth; or he can tell the truth, lose the girl and fortune, but serve the Higher Cause. Helped by his father's advice and prayers, Neal testifies truthfully and a grand jury soon indicts Barclay. Jeanette breaks with Neal who stalwartly finds work on a Chicago newspaper and continues to cherish her. But the Commerce Department has to present its case before Federal Judge Lige Bemis who, in spite of damning evidence, dismisses it out of hand. Still, the attendant negative publicity and the changes in public mood that indictment represents are the first real blows to John's cynical egoism and shake his faith in the power of sacrosanct materialism.

Soon Bemis retires from the federal bench, returns to Sycamore Ridge, and with his honorarium from Barclay buys the town's waterworks company. He acquires it cheaply because its franchise is up, it gets its water supply from the Old Mill Pond which health officials suspect is the source of recent typhoid outbreaks, and Bob Hendricks has as a result organized a campaign for municipal ownership. Bemis thinks he can blackmail Bob into dropping that campaign with evidence of General Hendrick's old forgery which he obtains from Barclay and with a letter from Molly Brownwell lost twenty years before which reveals she had once planned to desert her husband for Bob, her true love. Bob refuses to be blackmailed and stoically arranges his affairs, knowing Brownwell's emotional instability. Incensed by the letter, Adrian shoots him dead, then flees town at Molly's urging, though the murder appears a suicide. Bemis wins, but Barclay recognizes with horror that he helped kill his old friend. Still, his soul remains unchanged, so that retribution is inevitable. Jane contracts typhoid and dies.

Grieving but unyielding, John continues his belief in the "Gospel of Wealth," though his mother urges him to recant and seek absolution and Molly appeals to him not to sacrifice his daughter as he had her. Finally, moved by his daughter's misery, he undergoes a Carlylean epiphany:

The old negation was fighting for its own, and he was weary and broken and sick as with a palsy of the soul. For everything in him trembled. There was no solid ground under him. He had visited his material kingdom in the City, and had seen its strong fortresses and had tried all of its locks and doors, and found them firm and fast. But they did not satisfy his soul; something within him kept mocking them; refusing to be awed by their power, and the eternal "yes" rushed through his reason like a great wind. (402)

John can now work out his redemption: he gives the town a new waterworks; he slowly and honestly divests his holding company of all of its assets, leaving him with valueless watered stock; he sends his secret card files on all shady American politicians to the White House for Commerce Department use; then, with Molly's help, he reunites Jeanette and Neal. He is now poor and his aged mother happy. An epilogue reports the end of John's saga two years later when he drowns in the Old Mill Pond during spring flood while rescuing Trixie Lee, disreputable daughter of the leader of the free-state irregulars at the 1860 Battle of Sycamore Ridge.

In White's lifetime the Macmillan Company sold nearly 300,000 copies of *A Certain Rich Man*, then a remarkable sales record. Part of its appeal was as a straightforward tract for the times, a fictionalized treatment of the ethos of the Progressive Era. For that happy faith in the transcendence of meliorism is nowhere more baldly stated than in this novel: public opinion

is not substantial; it is not palpable. It may not readily be translated into terms of money, or power, or vital force. But it crushes all these things before it. When this public opinion rises sure and firm and strong, no material force on this earth can stop it. For a time it may be dammed and checked. For a day or a week or a year or a decade it may be turned from its channel; yet money cannot hold it; arms cannot hold it; cunning cannot baffle it. For it is God moving among men. Thus He manifests Himself in this earth. Through the centuries, amid the storm and stress of time, often muffled, often strangled, often incoherent, often raucous and inarticulate with anguish, but always in the end triumphant, the voice of the people is indeed the voice of God! (326)

While most contemporary reviewers thought those voices "rather heavy at times," they praised the novel for its background verisimilitude and epiclike sweep; some also criticized its loose structure and contrived denouement. The most perceptive of those was H. L. Mencken; in his review "The Last of the Victorians" he compared White's tendentious narrative to those of William M. Thackeray. In obvious imitation of Thackeray's showman in *Vanity Fair*, White's narrator hovers about ubiquitously to call attention self-consciously to the mechanisms of his tale. But Mencken considers the resemblance between White and Thackeray far deeper than style or structure; it is in White's "fundamental concepts, in his morality, in his attitude toward the phenomena of life." For both are sentimentalists, preaching renunciation and other Christian virtues, relying on appeals to the heart and lachrymal glands. But in that, he observes, White is also assertively American because "sentimentality is our national weakness, as bigotry is our national vice."[26]

God's Puppets

God's Puppets (1916), White's last collection of short stories, received deservedly mixed reviews. It consists of three long tales written over several years for the *Saturday Evening Post* plus one for *Collier's*, "fictionalized editorials" John D. McKee called them.[27] To these White added a wistful little essay about boys past and present originally written for the *Post*, "sugar coating to leave a pleasant taste in the mouth after the pill had been administered," so he wrote Frank Lloyd Wright, the Chicago architect and a friend.[28] In the *Autobiography* he remarks that he wrote those stories because he was stale on his second novel, which had proved refractory and occupied him on and off for eight years. The stories are variations on the theme he said he was developing in that novel, "that there are no material rewards for spiritual excellence, and no material punishment for spiritual dereliction" (446). His epigraph to the collection is a broader version of that statement: "All service ranks the same with God— / With God, whose puppets best and worst / Are we. There is no last nor first." The stories also reflect the narrative difficulties he was having with the novel: he had determined to write the "great American social problem novel," though the genre was in truth incompatible with his temperament. An inherent romantic, White was unable to display the subtle gradations of motive implicit in mundane humanity. Though he wanted to make that novel "not a struggle between black and white but between different shades of gray," he simply could not shade the two major characters, one a sinner and the other a saint, but made them unalloyed contrasts. Thus Vernon L. Parrington noted sadly, "there is something pathetic in the way the harmless bleating romantics were dragged at the chariot wheels of social problems. Booth Tarkington, Mary Johnston, Winston Churchill, William Allen White were sacrificed equally...."[29]

In *God's Puppets* each story is heavy with biblical overtones; each is an extended parable for the Preacher's pronouncement "vanitas vanitatum"—materialism ultimately brings emptiness. All four are set in the town of New Raynham and have interlocking characters. Though politics receive little emphasis here, the character conflicts come under the same subject umbrella as in the stories of *Stratagems and Spoils* some fifteen years before: personal morality impressed by Gilded Age values. In the third story, "A Prosperous Gentleman," the narrator observes, "The age had planted its shams; its false valuations; its meaningless architecture; its fortunes founded on fraud; its lies and cheats in religion; and its mawkish sentiment in art ... [the main character's] sordid choice in life's great decision between the ways of life was due to the age and its environing shams—for it was a material age and in it youth had few visions" (209). But on the whole the narrative is less intense than in *Stratagems and Spoils*, more similar to the tone of *In Our Town*, with the narrator a wise, ubiquitous participant in and observer of the affairs of New Raynham and with minor characters contributing to the telling of the story, including the newspaper editor Archimedes and members of his staff.

The first story, "A Social Rectangle," is about Lalla Rookh Longford, who in her sexual vanity enthralls first the young romantic Dr. Paul Kurtlin; then her husband, renowned physicist Gregory Nixon; and finally the socially awkward but virile newspaper reporter Jimmy Lawton. Events are related both by our omniscient narrator and by Elsie Barnes, the *Times-Globe* society editor. The plot explicates the insatiable soul of beautiful Lalla Rookh, an egocentric temptress who seeks excitement of sexual power amid the fixtures of wealth, and contrasts her values to those of Elsie, a plain girl who selflessly sticks by her man though his and her dependent parents delay marriage. Lalla neglects her children, brings shame to her father, and destroys her men. Though standard melodrama, the story attempts the theme of vanity unrestrained by an age of materialism. The next story is a long, simplistic exemplum on the evils of greed. Entitled "The One a Pharisee," it retells the parable of the Pharisee and the Publican through the lives of two stepbrothers, the sanctimonious banker Boyce Kilworth and the disreputable gambler Caleb Hale. Because his wife and son are shunned by respectable society, Caleb leaves town to strike it rich with a Cripple Creek gold mine but returns like the prodigal son apparently penniless to run a little flower shop, accepted by the town and quietly happy amid the intangible beauty of his plants. Meanwhile, behind a righteous mask, Boyce fraudulently heaps up wealth and garners public respect. Then after some years Caleb's son falls in love with Boyce's daughter only to become entangled in the criminal failure of the Kilworth bank. But Caleb comes to the rescue with the Cripple Creek fortune he had secretly buried behind his greenhouse. In a reversal of the parable of the talents White holds ethereal Caleb up as the faithful servant and materialistic Boyce as the wicked one.

Both "A Prosperous Gentleman" and "The Gods Arrive" are equally simplistic tales of human vanity. The first is a sentimental lesson about pride in which the wealthy banker Charley Herrington jilts a drayman's daughter in his youth only to have her memory haunt him in his senility. The latter traces the pathetic decline of conservative Congressman Joel Ladgett, a Kansas Mr. Micawber. After his defeat at the polls, he and his wife keep up a flimsy pretense of gentility and imminent return to power, though impoverished and politically anachronistic. Unable to face the reality of change, they persist for years with their pale illusion, living at a hotel owned by their old campaign manager, where they "help out some." Of the four stories in *God's Puppets* this last seems the most successful because it is the least pretentious. A reviewer for the *Springfield Republican* pointed to the shared flaw of the others when he wrote, "one feels that Mr. White is writing for the story-teller's effect rather than for conviction."[30]

The Martial Adventures of Henry and Me

In terms of publication date *The Martial Adventures of Henry and Me* (1918) is White's next book of fiction, fiction in narrative structure at least. Its subject is a six-week tour of the Western European war front that he and Henry Allen took on behalf of the American Red Cross. Given the complimentary rank of lieutenant colonels, they sailed for France August 1917, only four months after the United States' declaration of war, to gather firsthand impressions for their support of Red Cross publicity drives. In the *Autobiography* White remembered the origin of this book as Sallie's insistence, after his return to Emporia, that he take the letters he sent home and make a book of them, because they were impressions of the American war effort "hot off the griddle." That is disingenuous. The book occurred to him on shipboard outward bound; he wrote it not only to boost the war effort but also to draw attention to Henry Allen, for whom he planned a successful 1918 campaign for governor of Kansas; and in addition to the letters he used material from syndicated newspaper articles he wrote in November to publicize the work of the American Red Cross.[31] He finished the manuscript in January and Macmillan published it early in April.

Though White clearly intended the book as a period piece, it still retains an appeal to the casual reader because in it he assumed a humorous point of view reminiscent of the designed naiveté of Mark Twain's *Innocents Abroad*. Unlike Twain, however, White was not flippant. Nor did he rely on the unadorned charm of a kaleidoscope of the American male in sundry travel poses. Instead he invented a flimsy fiction about a romantic triangle to give suspense to his narrative. And he provided his sketches with structural continuity by an ongoing story of his and Henry's troubles with military uniforms and European formalities and by their contrasting critiques of Continental cookery. Throughout, his tone was mellow, his fun gently self-deprecating, his announced objective a modest attempt to instruct and entertain. White was to remember it in his autobiography as "a trivial book, and the theme of it was in the first paragraph: the story of two fat middle-aged men who went to war without their wives. I rigged up a rather cobwebby romance to give the book a backbone; I knew that sketches would not be read. But I felt that if the experiences I had enjoyed—and I really did enjoy them even though I was frightened—were hung on the thread of a tenuous love affair, the book would have a chance" (535). Aided by twenty-four caricatures by Tony Sarg, the narrative brought luck, for the book was an immediate success, selling nearly 50,000 copies in all.

Along with the purposeful buffoonery attached to "Henry and me,"

White reported the state of morale in the war zones as he and Allen toured Red Cross facilities. As publicist he describes the beginning deployment of American forces in France with particular reference to Red Cross organization and personnel, praising especially Major Grayson Murphy, European commissioner. That is conventional journeyman's work. More interesting is his thoughtful account of European wartime conditions in the late summer of 1917, in which he underscores the sacrifices by France and England and the effects of war upon social and moral order. Here he is a stereotypical American progressive as war brings dilemma and defeat. He sees and understands the socially destructive results of war but believes those results can be turned into moral good, proclaiming

all these things are temporary; with the war's passing they will pass. The real thing we found was an awakening people, coming into the new century eager and wise and sure that it held somewhere in its coming years the dawn of a new day. That really is the hope of the war—an industrial hope, not a political hope, not a geographical hope, but a hope for better things for the common man. It is a hope that Christianity may take Christendom, and that the fellowship among the nations of the world so devoutly hoped for, may be possible because of a fellowship among men inside of nations. (266)

But the progressives of both American parties sadly underestimated the ingrained power of European prejudices, which nullified the reforming spirit of Woodrow Wilson's Fourteen Points and which White began to fathom only as he covered the Peace Conference in 1919. And in America wartime anxiety and bigotry brought about postwar reaction and moral letdown, effectively blocking any ballasting of the derailed Progressive Movement. Such war-spawned hysteria, which defeated White's larger hope, is apparent in this his own account, for he naively retails German atrocity stories and judges the "Huns" as morally reprehensible. Thus, this is no "trivial book" in one important respect: it documents American hopes and spirits as we entered World War I and points up the pathos of the results.

In the Heart of a Fool

From 1910 through 1917 White worked ambitiously but intermittently at a long second novel about America's late nineteenth-century industrial revolution and its unfortunate social consequences.

During February and March 1918 he gave the manuscript a final revision, then sent it to the Macmillan Company, which published it in October under the title *In the Heart of a Fool*. In it he traces on a larger canvas than in *A Certain Rich Man* the same thematic conflict of transcendentalism versus materialism and fills the foreground with a similar yet larger array of social issues, but this time his novel was a distinct failure, receiving mixed reviews and selling poorly. Everett Rich, one of White's biographers, described the book as a "belated problem novel, appearing after the American people had lost their taste for political and economic reform" and tied its failure to the wartime decline of progressivism.[32] Bad timing indeed contributed to this novel's poor sales, but its failure with reviewers was due in large part to its own inherent flaws. In *A Certain Rich Man* White succeeded in giving the illusion of reality to conventional melodrama through a vivid panorama of place and time. That did not happen in *In the Heart of a Fool*. Though he gives his plot an authentic envelope of contemporary social conflict and thought, his failure here is in mimesis: his story does not convey the requisite illusion of reality. Francis Hackett, one of the editors of *New Republic*, exclaimed in a long, signed review: "Well, Mr. William Allen White, I admire your purpose, but I stumble over your novel.... I do not believe in novels when the people in those novels are crudely subordinated to the moral design of the creator. When morality comes in the door art flies out the window."[33] Hackett was too moderate with that metaphor: White dragged morality in by both doors, making design transparently subordinate to purpose and thereby failing to persuade his readers to suspend disbelief.

Paradoxically, the reason he failed to persuade was his didactic theory of fiction: he had come to consider the novel chiefly a vehicle for presenting philosophies of life. In a commentary he wrote in 1922 for a *New Republic* literary supplement about "The Novel of Tomorrow" he advocated a tolerant form of moral criticism, which he described as a democratic theory based on mutual respect, not rigid standards or inexorable rules. He believed novels should be for the day and that criticism should be a relative matter dependent on philosophical taste, "largely a question of the world in which the authors move, of the philosophy of life which inspires the writer."[34] Unfortunately for the success of *In the Heart of a Fool*, as judged by the reviews, most of its readers wanted more world and less philosophy. Some, like H. L. Mencken, wanted more art. In an article in

Smart Set he compared White's new novel to Willa Cather's *My Antonia* and exclaimed, "White's shows the viewpoint of a Chautauqua spell-binder and the manner of a Methodist evangelist. It is, indeed, a novel so intolerably mawkish and maudlin, so shallow and childish, so vapid and priggish, that its accumulated badness almost passes belief...." But then, as in his review of *A Certain Rich Man*, Mencken softened his attack by generalizing it: "after all, the book is absolutely American—that, for all its horrible snuffling and sentimentalizing, it is a very fair example of the sort of drivel that passes for 'sound' and 'inspiring' in our fair republic and is eagerly praised by the newspapers, and devoured voraciously by the people."[35]

Part of the problem with *In the Heart of a Fool* is setting. The novel takes place in the industrial town of Harvey situated in the "Wahoo Valley," somewhere between Kansas City and Omaha. That town is as much the subject of the novel as any of its characters, for White focused on the emergence of class conflicts and social inequities within a generation of the town's founding in rough democracy. But unlike Sycamore Ridge in *A Certain Rich Man*, important parts of Harvey are not imaginatively realized, because White portrays its laborers in amorphous hues against vague backgrounds. Not surprisingly, White wrote his best fiction about the side of life he knew firsthand. He had not lived with modern industrial conditions. Though he had spent several years in Kansas City, he was at that time a smug young journalist interested in poetry, Sallie Lindsay, and conservative Republican politics, not the social problems accompanying industrial development. In this novel, then, he had to project himself vicariously into the conditions of labor and was unable to do so with sufficient imaginative vigor to achieve a realistic presentation of the laboring classes comparable to his sure-handed drawing of middle-class life. He shows sympathy for labor, of course, but it is for, not with. We frequently step into the book and tobacco shop on Harvey's Market Street but only once into the Red Dog Saloon down in the Bottoms where the immigrant laborers live.

An even greater problem within this novel is White's representation of the two principal characters, Grant Adams and Thomas Van Dorn. He presents them too blatantly as archetypal contrasts. Grant is a Christ surrogate, a red-headed, blue-eyed, robust carpenter; Van Dorn is Mephistophelian, a black-haired, dark-eyed, suave corporation lawyer. Grant is the idealist, a truly selfless labor leader dedicated to a vision of brotherhood and social democracy. Van Dorn is the materialist, a ruthless tool of plutocracy who denies the reality of God to follow a creed of cynical hedonism. They are but tokens for the thesis of the novel, one he had expounded eight years earlier in his Columbia University speech, "A Theory of Spiritual Progress"— that there is no righteous retribution in the palpable form Job's friends expected, but that retribution comes nevertheless. The Peach-blow philosopher, an obtrusive narrative commentator, announces this theme several times; for instance:

Life disheartens us because we expect the wrong things of it. We expect material rewards for spiritual virtues, material punishments for spiritual transgressions; when even in the material world, material rewards and punishments do not always follow the acts which seem to require them. Yet the only sure thing in the world is that our spiritual lapses bring spiritual punishments, and our spiritual virtues have their spiritual re-wards. (288)

In animating that theme White makes his two chief female characters just as emblematic. Laura Nesbit is the blonde homemaker, Margaret Müller the brunette temptress; they are the two faces of Eve. The secondary figures, on the other hand, are much more realistic and sometimes breathe life into the novel, though they too are types. The most individual among them is the political boss Doctor James Nesbit, whom White patterned closely upon memories of his father. With others, such as the shopkeepers George Brotherton and Brun-hilde Herdicker, he captures the talk, the humor, and the rhythms of life in the Midwest.

On the whole, the novel is a patent melodrama through which White reenacts the social and moral conflicts of his generation as seen by a born-again political liberal. As a symbolic figure Tom Van Dorn mirrors a one-dimensional image of Judge Joseph Gary, for example, who helped break the 1894 Pullman strike, and Grant Adams of Eugene V. Debs, who led that strike. The covert struggle between Laura and Margaret pits long-established domestic values against chicly mutable ones. In abbreviated form the labor-capital con-frontations in Harvey re-create the bloody strife in 1899 at Coeur D'Alene, Idaho, or in 1912 at Lawrence, Massachusetts. Predictably, Hollywood made *In the Heart of a Fool* into a movie in 1920. But that movie, with its flashy theatrics and inordinate focus on the sexual conflicts of the story line, embarrassed and deeply disappointed White.[36] In the novel he had used sensationalism as a means to an end, not as an end itself. For he had covered bare-bones melodrama with a thick comforter of authorial commentary quilted with a philosophy sometimes wise, usually sentimental, always Christian. The book was a long fictional tract for the times written by a deeply sincere fifty-year-old progressive who had traveled his road to Damascus nearly twenty years before. But because the public was now traveling a new road in a different direction, this was to be his last serious attempt to preach through fiction the gospel of social reform. Perhaps he was subconsciously thinking that when he commented about Grant Adams toward the end of the novel:

It is the curse of dreamers that they believe that when they are convinced of a truth, they who have pursued it, they have only to pass out their truth to the world to remake the universe. But the world is made over only when the common mind sees the truth, and the common heart feels it. So the history of reform is a history of disappointment. The reform works, of course. But in working it does only the one little trick it is intended to do, and the long chain of incidental blessings which should follow, which the reformers feel must inevitably follow, wait for other reformers to bring them into being. So there is always plenty of work for the social tinker, and no one man ever built a millennium. For God is ever jealous for our progeny, and leaves an unfinished job always on the workbench of the world. (524–25)

"Teaching Perkins to Play"

During the summer of 1920 White planned a series of short stories for the *Saturday Evening Post*, which he intended eventually to collect in book form as was his wont. But he completed only one, early in the spring of 1921, which he then sent to George Lorimer, editor of the *Post*, writing him,

Here is a story which is the first of a series. I want to locate some vacation stories out in Estes Park, with about the same cast of characters, more or less as the "In Our Town" stories are of the same cast of characters, and with the same scenic background. They will probably come rolling about a month apart. . . . I want to write something about the modern young man and woman who are giving Parent Teacher Associations such chilling horrors. And incidentally I want to write about the good middle class, middle western people in their vacation hours, showing what they do and think when they play.[37]

The magazine published that story in its 6 August 1921 issue as "Teaching Perkins to Play." It departs significantly from his previous fiction insofar as it is domestic situation comedy told from the viewpoint of the pompous middle-aged banker and harassed father Percival Perkins. White aimed simply to amuse and took many details from his own family life. On doctor's orders Perkins rents a cabin in Estes Park, Colorado, for a summer's vacation and the story concerns his flustered reactions to various contretemps caused mostly by the children and the family dog during the train trip there.

After his daughter's death in May 1921 White abandoned the series, apparently because of painful personal associations. Three years later in several letters he mentions working on a novel based on a Mediterranean cruise the Whites took early in 1923 with their lifelong friends Mr. and Mrs. Victor Murdock. That "novel" did not materialize. "Teaching Perkins to Play" stands as his last published work of fiction.

Chapter Five

A Puckish Kansas Sage: Social Histories

During the presidential campaign of 1920 Warren G. Harding promised the nation a return to "normalcy." Hard upon that promise, contiguous waves of reaction swept the country, smashing the social and political hopes of the increasingly beleaguered progressives. For them "normalcy" came to mean the return of plutocracy. After a brief period of despondency White was able to view that smash from the patient perspective of middle age, tempered by experience, secure in his beliefs. In December 1920, just after Harding's election, he wrote Victor Murdock, publisher of the *Wichita Eagle* and a nationally prominent Progressive Republican, "I feel that our splurge from 1903 to 1914 was well worth while. We did get a lot of things done. Things that are well worth doing; things that are permanent. But I feel also that nobody much is paying attention to those things now."[1] Through the 1920s and into the 1930s White paid attention to those things, not as an ebullient publicist surfing with TR in a high sea of reform but as a lonely sentinel patrolling the sands at ebbtide ready to answer the question, "Watchman, how goes the night?" In doing so he purposefully took up the mantle of the old prophet, as balding but not so hopeful of miracles as Elisha. His final books, then, are those of the "Sage of Emporia," biographies and social histories which attempt to explain the phenomena of recent change and offer some hope for the future.

Some Cycles of Cathay

Two of those books are certifiably sage, being collections of university lectures, expressly modified and published to "make men think." The first of these consists of a series of four lectures White gave at the University of North Carolina during April 1925 as part of an endowed program on American citizenship. After their delivery he edited three of them for publication in the university-sponsored

Journal of Social Forces, then added a preface and postscript for the publication of all four by the university's press as the small book *Some Cycles of Cathay.*[2] In the preface White apologizes for cluttering his manuscript with "restrictions and qualifications" not in his lectures but deemed necessary for a wider academic audience. Nevertheless, he maintains,

the thesis of the book, when it is finally set forth, is fairly simple: that our country has passed through three major political cycles, The Revolutionary Cycle, The Anti-Slavery Cycle, and The Populist Cycle; each cycle more or less duplicating the other, and all three cycles being a part of a larger cycle of democratic growth in the peoples and governments controlled by the English speaking races. The thesis also would demonstrate that even those larger tribal cycles are a part of a still greater cycle of development known rather loosely as Christian civilization. (v–vi)

To appeal to the academic mind he should have cluttered this book with even more "restrictions and qualifications." For in it he is no Arnold J. Toynbee, carefully marshaling evidence to support the hypothesis that spiritual not materialistic forces rule the course of history; he is instead an evangelist, asserting such an hypothesis as fact in order to affirm undaunted faith in social progress.

Essentially, in this book White argues by means of highlights from American history the need for symbiosis between politics and Christian morality to achieve meaningful social progress. In brief, he assumes that the original revolutionary was the Nazarene Carpenter whose doctrine of the inherent dignity of man's spirit, succinctly proclaimed in the Golden Rule and the Beatitudes, sowed the seeds of Western democracy. Those seeds quickened in the fertile social soil of Great Britain's Atlantic colonies to bloom thrice so far in American history, the last flowering being the Populist movement. White surveys that movement in his fourth chapter, which because of his unique historical interpretation is the most interesting section of the book. For example,

The "Roosevelt politics" put into terms of definite issues most of [the] vision for justice which lies at the heart of the American people. It is Populism up to 1912. As Roosevelt's influence waned, Wilson's came. And, because Bryan had impregnated the Democratic Party with Populism, and because Roosevelt had split the Republican Party over Populism, Wilson from 1913 to 1917 wrote into the statutes of our country many

of those aspirations of an earlier day. Yet they were so obviously Rooseveltian that Wilson had small credit for them. (82–83)

At the end of his survey White recognizes the present postwar years
are "dull days of futile reaction," but he catechizes, "Is it not pre-
sumable that democracy and its ideals are established to gather men
into some vast unity for another fight?" To which he responds opti-
mistically,

Surely these impassioned voices crying across our times for justice, surely
all this clanging of machinery, all this hiving in industry, all this organizing of commerce, all this levelling up of democracy, all the aspirations
of the prophets of our age for the natural rights of man and the call of
brotherhood that have been massing men by millions over the earth with
a common mind and a quickening heart, surely these signs and wonders
are portents of a new order. (95–96)

The Changing West

The other collection of modified university lectures, *The Changing
West: An Economic Theory About Our Golden Age*, was from a
series of three White delivered at Harvard University in April 1939
under the auspices of its Department of American History. There he
was the house guest of university president James B. Conant, to whom
he wrote later, "I am sending herewith on this mail a copy of a book
that I made out of my Harvard lectures plus an article in the *Yale
Review* plus another article in the *Survey Graphic* which I wrote
while I was thinking about the subject which was assigned for my
talks at Harvard."[3] That volume represents his final hortatory analysis of the development of American civilization north of the Ohio
River and west of the Alleghenies clear to the Pacific. It differs slightly
in specifics but not in theory from his many previous analyses. For
in that book he emphasizes the spiritual and political inheritance of
the pioneers of the nineteenth century, a phylogenic Protestant and
democratic heritage which proved the catalyst for synthesizing the
vast untapped resources of Western lands into great wealth widely
distributed. White theorizes that the opportunity for that unique
"democratic capitalism" occurred because land values rose dramatically during the settlement of the West, a rise caused by the intelligent labor of free and literate men. The result was increments of
surplus wealth used by those men to create more wealth, ultimately

for the common good, testimony to the power of Christian ethics and universal education as taught in the country church and the village school. According to White "those were the two basic free institutions—the church and the school—upon which the West was built, a unique civilization in the earth, a new thing for mankind" (13).

Corruption, of course, was part of that new civilization because man is acquisitive as well as altruistic, "but the net of it, which gave the West its glory, was good—as good as man!" (21). And this good continues because that wide distribution of wealth established middle-class rule, to the benefit of the entire nation. For it was the middle-class virtues of courage, honesty, charity, and intelligence that within this century successfully stalemated the dominance of plutocracy, with the result that middle-class liberalism is now "the strongest single political force in the United States" (45). But in the hard times of the 1930s White believes, such endemic liberalism is endangered by a "dour radicalism" which advocates either the "totalitarian philosophy of state capitalism" or a "dictatorship of the proletariat." He warns that "for a catastrophic decade, western middle-class democracy founded upon the Christian ethic and grounded in capitalism has stood like a rock. But like a rock our democratic capitalism has forces beneath it which slowly are eating into a place where the rock may shift and veer if it does not tumble" (57). He sees the eroding economic base of the Western farmer as that vulnerable place.

In the past, according to White, rising land values established unrealistic economic expectations sustained by a lengthy war boom. Those expectations encouraged the farmer to borrow incautiously to mechanize his life-style, increase his budget, and destroy his previously self-sufficient way of life. But now land values have stabilized and boom times are over. The farmer finds himself tied to the volatile economic cycles of an industrialized world and "must rise or fall upon the purchasing power of the industrial worker." Consequently, the drastic worldwide financial slump has so curtailed the Western farmer's own purchasing power that he is in danger of falling to tenant farmer status to think and vote like a peasant. But White believes that the farmer will not suffer himself to be thus declassed. Because he holds the political national balance of power, the farmer's problems will continue to occupy the attention of the American Congress until it finds a solution.

It must find a solution, White insists, because Western middle-class liberalism is fundamental to the well-being of American democracy. But he is hopeful: he believes that under FDR the nation has already gone far in remedying the mistakes of the 1920s and is now thinking in new social, political, and economic terms. Still, White cautions against going too far too fast because that will bring reaction once again. He suggests instead a greater reliance on gradualism and less on massive, sweeping state programs, for "the political lesson of the last trek westward of the American people in the nineteenth century and the first decades of the new century is to trust evolutionary processes inherent in our democracy" (105). Those processes may even "hold science in the ways of justice" and at the same time maintain the "essential freedom of enterprise and invention" necessary to the continuing success of an industrialized democracy (114). Thus at age seventy-one, at the end of five decades of commenting on the passing scene, William Allen White continued to insist that the fusion of the Protestant ethics with Anglo-Saxon freedoms is the key to America's singular social history and to optimism about its destiny.

Woodrow Wilson

In 1919 White returned from the Paris Peace Conference with great faith in Woodrow Wilson's ideals and hesitant admiration for his leadership. Though he never lost that faith, he soon lost that admiration, repelled by the president's self-defeating, petty intransigency that allowed a small group of Senate isolationists to block American approval of the Versailles Treaty and the League of Nations. As a Bull Mooser, White had opposed Wilson's candidacy in 1912 and 1916 yet in general supported the social legislation of his first term and the wartime diplomacy of the second, an ambivalent pattern White repeated with FDR, even to puzzlement over the man's personality. But with those two he was puzzled by nearly opposite traits, bemused on one hand by FDR's cheerful expediency and on the other by Wilson's aloof, sometimes grim stubbornness, a character flaw that turned the final days of his administration into a tragedy of dashed hopes. Committed to those hopes and deeply distressed by that tragedy, White ultimately viewed Wilson as both hero and villain, a dichotomy he captured in a famous four-line editorial written when Wilson died early in 1924, an embittered, partially paralyzed old man. "God gave him a great vision. / The devil gave him an imperious heart. / The proud heart is still. / The vision lives."[4] That was the view White developed in the biography published in September of that year as *Woodrow Wilson: The Man, His Times and His Task.*

In method and purpose that book is but an extended version of the magazine sketches he had been writing since 1900. It too is an impressionistic interpretation of the manners and morals of a prominent politician, set within his social and political context and viewed in terms of his values. Soon after publication, White wrote a friend: "The Wilson book was a labor of love. I disliked the man tremendously, but was rather fond of his type."[5] Intrigued by the man, by his great promise and potential for failure, he accepted a commission late in 1919 from the Houghton Mifflin Company to do the Wilson volume for a projected Modern American Statesmen series, though he would rather have done the book for the Macmillan firm, to which he remained loyal the rest of his life.[6] But delayed by other projects and the trauma of his daughter's death, he did not work seriously on the volume until the fall of 1923. Early in 1924 he interviewed a select number of Wilson's friends and enemies, his standard technique of data gathering, to base much of his assessment on heredity and early environment, his standard touchstones for determining character. Thus in the book he presents Wilson as a Scotch-Irishman with a Southern genteel Presbyterian heritage and a vigorous academic mind who catapulted into the White House untempered by the give and take of a rough boyhood or a tough political apprenticeship. He ascribes much of Wilson's formidable personality to an awkward genetic blend of the dour Scotch Woodwards with the mercurial Irish Wilsons. In Wilson the boy that uneasy blend, in reaction with sheltered circumstances, formed a curiously defensive, hubristic temperament that led ultimately to his self-defeat and its sad implications for the world.

As an active political participant, reporter, and commentator White had followed Wilson's career from the time he was elected governor of New Jersey in 1910 to his death and was well acquainted with several of his closest associates—Robert S. Bridges, Ray Stannard Baker, Colonel Edward M. House, and Joseph P. Tumulty—in addition to some of his bitterest enemies. Prominent among the American press corps at the Peace Conference, White gained from his many contacts there, especially from the English reporter Norman Angell, a perspective that gave him a more sophisticated view of Wilson's Parisian efforts, obstacles, and successes than that of most American commentators. Wilson had even selected him, along with George Herron, to represent the United States at the tangential Prinkipo conference. Then during the 1919–20 battle in the Senate White was in the trenches as an uncommissioned officer fighting for the Treaty and the League. He had close friends as participants on both sides and knew at first hand how Wilson had snatched defeat out of the jaws of victory. So he drew much of the background for his biography from his own observations and, with Sallie's help, finished it quickly during the summer of 1924 in time for the fall market.

In the introduction he warned readers he had not compiled a source book or a documented "official" biography but offered instead a knowledgeable reporter's impressions of the man and his dream: "The story will disclose no new events nor details nor circumstances in the life of Woodrow Wilson, but perhaps the arrangement of our biographical material may help his contemporaries to a better understanding of him and his work" (ix). Two later biographies of Wilson are thoroughgoing scholarly works—Ray S. Baker's Pulitzer prize-winning *Woodrow Wilson: Life and Letters* (1927–39) and Arthur S. Link's definitive *Wilson* (1947–65)—so White's disclaimer is now especially true: his book is of little import as biography. In fact, it never was, due to his simplistic insistence on a hereditary source for Wilson's complex personality. But in tone and background it is an interesting social document, for it both lauds and debunks Wilson, revealing a perplexed love-hate relationship on White's part common to many disheartened progressives after the War.

In the book White assumes a familiar, even pert attitude toward his subject, as if to confute the austere public image of the wartime President. For it is "Tommy" Wilson during the early years—a frail, overprotected preacher's son and a lonely, occasionally petulant dreamer. White emphasizes the effects of that childhood on the youth and man; for instance, he notes that as a student at Princeton "Tommy" avoided participating in contact sports but made a good team manager; barely placed in the upper third of his class but read avidly and edited the school newspaper; was a popular collegian but on his own terms. That is the pattern White traces throughout Wilson's life, irreverently and often cleverly. Speaking of Wilson's brief tenure as a young professor at Byrn Mawr, for example, White observes:

He tried to make his lectures interesting. But politics, American history, and economics were not subjects that appealed greatly to young women of that day. And if Woodrow Wilson did not do a casual thing well enough to succeed and to prove his success by the approval of his kind, he would inevitably quit it. Anything but neglect might be borne with humility by a Wilson. But neglect, indifference, mere tolerance—a classroom of drooping, yawning girls, with here and there a bluestocking rampant—these were not for the son of his father. (108–9)

Another instance is at the start of his chapter about Wilson's professorial years at Princeton, for White begins with an unexpected demurrer, then qualifies it: "All his life Woodrow Wilson's major delusion was that he had a first-class mind. Tommy in the library with the old Doctor, suddenly bursting forth with the confession that he had a first-class mind, seems to have erected one of the stumbling blocks of Woodrow Wilson's career. What he had was a clear, clean, strong brain that was inadequately supported by a frail body. Always the brain was active" (120). On the whole, White's attitude is flippant but friendly; by that means he places Wilson firmly in the realm of the human where to err is. For his real objective is understanding, not wit, an objective that Claude G. Bowers, historian and journalist, granted White in a review of the book in the *New York World*, where he pronounced White's estimate of Wilson "fair, and probably true."[7]

More important to us are, first, White's authoritative insight into the American political process and, second, the emphasis he as a typical Midwestern liberal gives to Wilson's inspirational appeal as a wartime president, then peacemaker. White's purpose in the book is to assess personality; thus only a bit more than half covers Wilson's public life which contains little about his administrative record. For in that last half White focuses upon Wilson's abilities as a politician and attributes the man's early success but ultimate failure to political inexperience augmented by an impatient personality. White sees him as politically lucky, not astute. After being elected governor of New Jersey, for instance, he threw in with the reformers of his party because the times were right and he was uncommitted to the New Jersey machine, though its candidate. In 1912 Roosevelt bolted the Republicans, splitting the party. The Democrats deadlocked in convention, then nominated Wilson pretty much as a dark horse. So he was elected president almost by default and only by a plurality. In spite of his being elected to a second term, White points out, he never really understood the practical art of politics. Insufficiently aware that politics was more emotional than logical, impatient with patronage and palaver, unconcerned about rapport with Congress, distracted by foreign affairs, Wilson never earned the leadership of his party, White believes, though capable at times of great charisma. Consequently, in the crucial fight with the Senate "irreconcilables" he did not observe the rules of practical politics and suffered defeat. An old stager, White spoke to this point with authority.

As a leading Midwestern publicist he also knew what he was talking about when he observed that the West was "tremendously sentimental," which accounted for the region's positive response when Wilson shifted his slogan justifying America's entrance into the war from "freedom of the seas" to "making the world safe for democracy." Earlier in the book he inadvertently revealed that his own liberalism was based on sentiment rather than reason when he detailed the theoretical differences between TR's "New Nationalism" and Wilson's "New Freedom" then characterized those differences as "that fantastic imaginary gulf that always has existed between tweedledum and tweedle-dee" (264). Moral attitude appealed to him, not constitutional theory or administrative organization. Later, when assessing Wilson's role at the Peace Conference, he demonstrates that the Progressive Movement as a whole was an emotion, a state of mind, whose finest expression, he believes, was the moral spirit with which Wilson brought America into the war and to the peace talks. Thus White stops his narration of those talks to comment

Just here it is necessary to define the American idea which President Wilson brought with him—the vision which he would have realized. For, after all, our President was not important as a man, but as a representative of an ideal in connection with the story of the Peace Conference. As a man always he was remote, sometimes vague and never very interesting in Paris. But the ideal he took there was dynamic, and he cherished it and impersonated it well. It was the ideal of faith; faith in humanity, faith in the moral government of the universe, faith in the power of the spiritual forces of life to triumph over the material powers that be. He believed that reason, being the will of God, would prevail in international affairs if a reasoning place could be set up for international usage. Hence he stood for a League of Nations as a divinely appointed institution. (383)

As White views those talks, the cynical politicians of Europe, especially the French, took advantage of Wilson's personal and political weaknesses to outmaneuver him on the final treaty, then a few obstructionists at home traded on those same weaknesses to thwart Senate acceptance of the League. Obstinately refusing to compromise, Wilson decided to take his case to the people who, unknown to him in his self-imposed political isolation, had grown weary of the ideal. The rigors and frustrations of that tour, White believes, brought on the stroke and with it Wilson's final defeat, a defeat that encompassed the ideal itself. A true progressive, White ends his assessment of that debacle with the brave sentiment, "If it were not for the world's tragedies, men would lose their faith!" (460). Clearly, the Wilson biography was for White a work of love, a tribute not so much to the man but to what he stood for. In addition it is an interesting contemporary assessment of a major historical figure. In *A History of American Biography* Edward H. O'Neill said of White's study: "Considering the date of the book, it must be admitted that the author succeeded, as well as any man could at that time, in interpreting the complexities of character that went to the making of the war president."[8]

Calvin Coolidge and A Puritan in Babylon

In 1924, shortly after the American electorate confirmed Calvin Coolidge's presidency, George Lorimer of *Collier's* asked White to write one of his typical magazine sketches about that strange man in the White House. That sketch became a group of six that White then turned into a book-length biography, published in November 1925 by the Macmillan firm, under the title *Calvin Coolidge: The Man Who Is President.* That December White wrote a Kansas friend to explain what led to his compiling a book about a taciturn political stand-patter he had described in an early 1924 editorial as "the apotheosis of safety first": "Collier's Weekly wanted an article about Coolidge. I went east to get it without much thought of him, merely to fill an order, got interested in him, was baffled by him, and bedeviled by his evanescent character, wrote four articles then made it six, then concluded there was a book in it. . . ."[9] As he did for many of the portraits in the later *Masks in a Pageant*, White edited the articles for format and style but did not rewrite them. The book, therefore, has the virtues and faults of his magazine sketches. Hastily written for a popular audience, it is based on his own considerable knowledge of politics, on easily available published accounts of Coolidge, and on hearsay gleaned from a selection of his friends and associates. In the introduction White pronounced the book a limited study of an important contemporary personality, and reviewers commended it as such, with the notice in *Review of Reviews* ending, "Like all of Mr. White's writings, this sketch is honest, straightforward and interesting throughout."[10]

As in his study of Wilson, White emphasized Coolidge's heritage and career as the means for understanding his moral character. His background and character were so different from Wilson's, though, that White apparently became fascinated by the contrast, especially since he believed it reflected the postwar change in national mood. Coolidge seemed to epitomize the commonplace lawyer-politician, an unimaginative hack slowly working his way up through local and state offices to a governorship, then by chance assuming the presidency. But White decided that "Silent Cal" was most uncommon, a scrupulously honest advocate of plutocracy who dedicated his life to a belief in the sacramental nature of public service but was too backward to speak of it, a provincial Yankee mystic. Later, from the perspective of the Great Depression, White on his own initiative wrote a second biography of Coolidge in which he attempted to explain the temporary prosperity and false euphoria of the Coolidge Era. That book is a carefully researched study of the man and his times entitled *A Puritan in Babylon: The Story of Calvin Coolidge* (1938). It is White's most serious attempt at biography qua social history and remains today one of the standard works on Coolidge. Not so the first book, which Coolidge scholar Donald R. McCoy describes by comparison as "less factual, less critical, and less interesting."[11] That of course is by contrast; when written it was a timely, candid sketch of a strangely reticent president.

White begins that sketch with the assertion "Calvin Coolidge is an enigma, not an accident" (8). He explains that enigma, and the mood of the American people who elected it, by showing how Coolidge's rise was not by chance but the result of character traits that matched tendencies of the times. Thus to White Coolidge is no mystery but a crossword puzzle requiring only time and effort to fill out. A puzzle is the controlling metaphor for this sketch, with the answer found in the president's remark that "No Coolidge ever went

West." For White believes the key is Coolidge's Vermont upbringing with its emphasis on the seven cardinal virtues of silence, economy, caution, honesty, industry, sincerity, and idealism. These are the traits of Coolidge the office holder, "poor as Job's turkey and proud as Lucifer" with an "ambition for public service, not for his own sake but for the public good as he saw it—a real patriot right out of the fourth-reader stories and alas, perhaps, sometimes liable to fourth-reader limitations" (85–86). The gist of those limitations, as White views the man, is his almost pathological caution, for he has "precious little aspiration, no urge to adventure, no yearning for larger liberties, no vision of nobler living" (216). But those very negations appealed to the national electorate, White believes, because such self-centered caution typifies the postwar era. Though White describes Coolidge as a lukewarm liberal on political issues during the Progressive Era, he notes the president always regarded the first order of government to be the fostering of business, even over social justice. So now he represents the mainstream of American sentiment: "Now after the World War, this was the American attitude—this belief in the sacrosanct quality of business in life" (237).

In this first sketch White is concerned foremost with the political man, with his abilities, his style, his moral character, and, through them, his potential as president. He finds him consistent, sincere, and scrupulously honest but without that "quality of daring that makes a great leader," for he has no warmth, no vision, no aura of command. Because of that he is unable so far to control his own Republican Congress and as the result conservative Senator Charles Curtis of Kansas and liberal Senator William Borah of Idaho, both Republicans and friends of White's, have assumed actual legislative leadership. The book consists of five parts nearly equal in length: in the last two White sketches the careers of those two men as contrasts to the president's in order to point up the situation in Washington and offer a prognosis for the rest of that administration. Indeed, White devotes a relatively small proportion of the book to biographical data, concentrating instead on the causes and political effects of Coolidge's personality. In general his assessment of the man is critical but sympathetic, softened in part by his respect for Coolidge's honest steadiness of character.

The second biography is more critical, conveying a tone of sympathy but not respect for its subject. In it he depicts Coolidge as a small-souled, narrow-minded man whose universe was fenced "horse high, hog tight and bull strong around the citadel of prosperity," yet a man who "played a clean game with the run of the dirty cards" (99). White started the book in 1933, after the death of Coolidge, as an explanation, so he told a friend, "of the development of our plutocracy from McKinley's administration into an organized, arrogant, self-conscious governing oligarchy in 1929, the span of Coolidge's political life."[12] Interviewing more of Coolidge's friends more thoroughly, he worked on it off and on for five years, delaying completion nearly two years to hire a researcher to wade through the unpublished letters of William Howard Taft which the family granted White access to in 1936 and which he used extensively to give color to the Washington years. The Macmillan Company issued it in November 1938 and by the end of December it was in a fifth printing. White's son thought it his father's most important book from the standpoint of scholarship and research, and contemporary reviewers heartily agreed, including such eminent historians as Matthew Josephson, Arthur M. Schlessinger, and Walter Millis. In fact, in a recent assessment of prominent historians' negative attitudes towards Coolidge, Thomas B. Silver asserted in the *American Scholar* that "it is White's biography of Coolidge, more than any other, that has molded subsequent opinion about the man."[13]

As in the sketches, he used recurrent allusions for thematic continuity, comparing Coolidge to a museum piece and to Cinderella, alluding often to his prissy walk and pursed mouth and emphasizing his egocentric avoidance of responsibility by repeating his youthful disclaimer "It wa'n't my stove." But, unlike the sketches, he bolstered and greatly expanded historical background with a spectrum of references from published commentaries and memories, from data winnowed out of newspaper files and public records by several research assistants, and from wide-ranging conversations with former official and unofficial power brokers, such as Herbert Hoover, secretary of commerce under Coolidge, and "Ike" Hoover, White House head usher. And he gave the events of Coolidge's life a much wider perspective by prefacing each of the four sections of the book with a brief survey of contemporaneous European history as "a sort of obligato to the American story" and by comparative references in the text to other current American events. The result was a scholarly historical biography, sprightly written and well-documented. Its emphasis on recent socioeconomic history White clearly announced in a long general preface.

In this book White indicts the Coolidge Era as one of moral and economic madness in which all Christendom had a Chamber of Commerce complex, that "was and is fundamentally creative, instinctively geared to grapple economic problems of production, in a day and a time when invention should have been contriving improvements with distributive systems" (395). He points out that Coolidge himself was but a freakish symbol of that mad carnival, a man whose "thin, dry, harsh personality" the age dramatized into a myth that masked the perversities of the times, a puritan in Babylon. Though he cleaned the Ohio gang out of the White House, he let in a crew of Big Business moguls "smartly frock-coated, plug-hatted, high-collared, bespatted and smuggly proud . . . which was to devastate his country more terribly than Harding's greasy playfellows" (294). Though his frugal life-style testified to a commendable personal honesty, publicly he supported property's controlling and profiting from the political process, as shown, for instance in his ignoring Justice Taft's attempts to upgrade appointments to the federal bench. Against the cautionary advice of Commerce Secretary Herbert Hoover and many banking officials, he followed Treasury Secretary Andrew W. Mellon, his "bad angel," in a policy of easy money and official pronouncements of optimism, which fueled an already overheated stock market, to Mellon's own advantage White suggests.

All in all, he presents Calvin Coolidge as "a puzzled, befuddled small-town New Englander torn with inner conflict while he turned to the world a smooth, flinty, unrevealing face," content to be "an attitude rather than an executive" (371). And that is the gist of his story. Coolidge was no hero; he "only typified his country, the ruling class, the middle class, honest, earnest, hard-working" optimists blindly following the god Prosperity. Thus, White asserts, it is neither honest nor intelligent to judge him by "the perspective of another decade that his wisdom may be questioned"; nevertheless, we should still remember in reviewing his lack of action that he "was never without access to the truth" (386). Because of his ethical egoism, he chose not to seek it and thereby disdained responsibility—"it wa'n't his stove"—which damned the man, so White implies, along with his era.

The Autobiography

The Autobiography of William Allen White, published posthumously in 1946, is a vivid tapestry of America's Gilded Age and

Progressive Era woven by an exuberant participant from an uncommonly frank and tolerant point of view. It is an invaluable piece of Americana. He worked on it during his last three years, while in his mid-seventies, after resigning as chairman of the Committee to Defend America by Aiding the Allies, but even then he could not bring himself to focus on that one task, though his health was increasingly uncertain and it was a long-cherished project. With the *Gazette* staff cut by war, he spent more time at the office and, of course, did not ignore Kansas politics or his long-standing commitment to the Book-of-the-Month Club. When he knew death was imminent, he greatly regretted not finishing, having traced events up to mid-spring 1923. At his request his son edited the unfinished manuscript for publication, then wrote a brief postscript covering the last two decades. Widely reviewed and praised, the book was a best-seller and won the Pulitzer prize for biography in 1947. The journalist Will Irwin, his career contemporaneous with White's, remarked in the *Saturday Review of Literature*: "Nothing else I know in American literature gives so effectively the feeling of a West just emerging from the pioneer period as the earlier chapters, nothing more fully the merits and limitations of small-city life and the meanness of small-city politics as the middle part, and when he comes to the era when national politics absorbed his best energies he adds many an important page to the authentic record of the times."[14]

White once noted that in writing an autobiography a man is prone to rationalize his conduct after the fact, the extent of "which helps to run the boundaries of a man's vanity."[15] His own vanity was well within bounds, for he starts with the warning that his tale is necessarily fiction, not to be confused with reality, no matter how close it may seem to correspond. That was wise, for he was an old man recounting the significant events of a busy life, knowing full well that memory and fact are sometimes tangential. But, he assures us, he is trying his best "to set down some facts which seem real and true" to him. Because reality depends more on selection and interpretation than on strict accuracy of detail, we cannot ask for a better disclaimer.

Sometimes, he does misremember events, but we know it does not matter much because his tone throughout is that of a salty truthfulness. For example, he tells how, after he took over the *Gazette*, Monday, 3 June 1895, his competitor Charles Eskridge of the *Republican* greeted him Tuesday with the two-line item "Will A. White, of Kansas City, has bought the Gazette from W. Y. Morgan. Next!"

(263). That is not so. Eskridge wrote a more fulsome and friendlier greeting:

The Gazette, a paper published in this city, has just changed hands, W. Y. Morgan retiring and Will A. White stepping into his shoes. Judging from the valedictory of the one and the salutatory of the other they are both happy. How this can be is a question that would puzzle a naturalist, but it appears to be so. Mr. Morgan and the editor of this paper always got along amicably and we trust the same feelings may prevail during the editorial life of his successor. . . . He is one of the brightest young men of the State and we welcome him to Emporia with hospitable hands in this his first venture to go it alone.[16]

Of course, the success of that young man soon changed Eskridge's patronizing attitude to that of angry scorn, which was the reality White remembered. Likewise, the years blurred small details. In recounting the background of "What's the Matter with Kansas?" he says he wrote it on Saturday, 13 August; in 1896, 13 August was a Thursday. In 1912 his contract with the Adams syndicate to cover the national conventions was for $1,200, not $1,000 per convention (461). He covered the 1919 Peace Conference for the Wheeler, not the McClure syndicate (550). Only one of the short stories he projected in 1920 was published and by the *Saturday Evening Post*, not "some of them" in the *Post* and *Collier's* (592). Such mistakes seem but tricks of the mind; had he lived he may well have caught some of them in manuscript. For Paul A. Jones, editor of the *Lyons Daily News*, declared in a tribute to White after his death: "Of all his talents, the most amazing to me was his remarkable memory. He never forgot anything. . . ."[17]

Other discrepancies, though, do reveal the vanity of rationalization. For example, in his account of the Progressive party convention in Chicago in 1916 he remembers, dramatically, that he and his friends had not known of the direct telephone line from George Perkins's room at the Blackstone Hotel to TR's library in Oyster Bay until late in the convention, Friday afternoon, 9 June. By then, he implies, TR had decided to refuse nomination because of a slanted picture of the "situation" conveyed by Perkins and his coterie (524–26). Stenographic transcriptions of calls on that line show otherwise. TR knew full well what he was doing when he refused nomination and killed the party. Perkins was only following Roosevelt's wishes, which White could not but realize from his own phone conversations with TR on that line Friday evening and night. But he undoubtedly knew that before the convention met, just as he must have known about the private phone line, which, according to Perkins's biographer John A. Garraty, "was front-page news even before the opening of the conventions."[18] Still, White blames Perkins for TR's ambivalent statement of rejection Saturday, the last day of the convention. Apparently, Will could not accept, even after many years, the reality of Roosevelt's conduct on that occasion. Nor his own in 1920: in thinking back to that national election, he cannot remember supporting editorially the Republican ticket of Harding and Coolidge (596). Yet he did so in six separate editorials in the *Gazette* during September and October of that year.[19]

Seemingly more disingenuous is his explanation for two misleading, prominently by-lined articles about Thunder Mountain gold mines that he placed in a specious mining journal in 1903–4. He writes:

I was cautious enough in my Post articles, though [*sic*] I told the truth about the unsolved difficulties. Then one day along came an offer from what looked to me like a reputable mining journal in New York for two thousand dollars for another article about Thunder Mountain. I wrote it, and was amazed and ashamed—ashamed that I should have been such a sucker and ashamed of my profession when I read the article in that mining paper which had entirely distorted my viewpoint.... I narrowly escaped disgrace. Only luck and the fact that I answered scores of letters denouncing what the mining journal had done kept me from real trouble.... (367–68)

On the contrary, White's letters to Lewis Van Riper, mine owner and journal editor, reveal that Will regarded him a good friend, was personally involved in his speculations, and initiated the article: "My Dear Van: I wrote to you some time ago about ten thousand dollars worth of Crown property shares and that I would be glad to pay for it with a 1,000 [*sic*] article for your United States Mining Journal...."[20] Three years later, after that Idaho gold boom had collapsed and that journal ceased, he wrote an embarrassed letter to Van Riper asking him if he could clarify some of their stock transactions from his office records and also send him a copy of the original articles because "some fellows who hate me in politics are trying to make it appear ...

that there was something irregular in the fact that I went to Thunder Mountain with you to write for the Journal."[21] White's brief and indignant disclaimer nearly forty years after those events is sophistic in its implications, but to what extent consciously so is, of course, moot. In fact, the impression that emerges from a random comparison of his memoirs to his voluminous letter files is that such clear-cut instances of rationalization are relatively few. The vanity inherent to autobiography does seem in this one under healthy control.

In structure and style the autobiography is vintage White. Felicitous in diction, crisp in syntax, the story is told by a master journalist secure in his trade. If style reveals the man himself, then White had a large and happy soul. As in all his previous sketches, he emphasizes in this the formation of character through the interaction of inheritance, heritage, and environment. Likewise, he reiterates shibboleths to emphasize his thematic structure—such as, "the job of a good citizen is to make his private opinion public opinion" (369)—and repeats variations on figures of speech inherent to his theme—such as "I thought I was bearing down heavily on an Archimedean lever that was moving my world," but instead "I was a bubble on a swiftly moving current" (399). But scholastic rhetorical analysis cannot do justice to the rich narrative flow. The book must be read to be appreciated, for it is truly a "recreation of self." Related from a mellow and at the same time puckish old age, it embodies a person whose writings and activities, humor and idealism enriched national life nearly fifty years. Although Will White did not take himself very seriously, he believed unabashedly in serious things—in love, faith, charity, justice, honesty—and he captured that playful righteousness, a rare combination, in this his life's story.

Chapter Six

The Voice of the Midwestern Middle Class: An Assessment

To millions of Americans in the third and fourth decades of this century, William Allen White was more than a well-known journalist and Progressive Republican. He was a public "personality," a widely acknowledged embodiment of Midwestern, middle-class, small-town, moderately liberal public opinion. It was a role he had sedulously cultivated. To the extent he was accepted in that role, he had attained his life's ambition, an ambition he proclaimed in 1895 in his first editorial for the *Gazette*. He had set out, he wrote, to make the private opinion of "the good, honest, upright, God-fearing, law-abiding people" of his community public opinion because "public sentiment is the only sentiment that prevails."[1] Throughout his life he maintained great faith in the melioristic power of public opinion, properly applied. That faith is the key to his sometimes puzzling behavior and somewhat diffuse career.

White was an Emersonian Christian who believed that humanity advances only insofar as each of us discerns and upholds the spiritual purpose of the universe. To him mankind's continued progress depends not on legislated morality mechanically imposed upon the community but instead on community ethics organically imprinted upon the individual. In his early lecture "A Theory of Spiritual Progress" he asked himself "What is the prod that ever keeps mankind going in a given direction?" He answered: "Let us suppose that sin and evil or whatever we may call life's somber forces that make for pain or unhappiness or sorrow, are infractions of the social code. Whatever else the social code may be—it is the sum of the customs of the people; it has public sentiment behind it; it is more powerful than any human law. Whoever violates public sentiment . . . feels the disapproval of his neighbors. That disapproval is a basis for the conviction of sin."[2] Since consciousness is sensibility, any such person must feel "the grind of public sentiment" upon him and, following

124

the course of least resistance, gradually conform to the ways of society. "Through the sensibilities of humanity, kindness grows. Thus the race moves from the material world into the spiritual" (15). The publicist, then, has a divine mission: he furthers the "way of the Lord" by creating and focusing public sentiment.

White believed with buoyant optimism in man's innate goodness and mankind's inevitable progress: "here and now we find the divine light in man. The upward growth of mankind is hardly disputed" (7). Likewise, he believed that man's sensibilities were his link to the spiritual. Thus he predicated his espousal of reform on the assumptions that society changes for the better only insofar as the individual changes and the individual changes as his attitudes change, not through force but by appeals to his sense of brotherhood, to his emotional acceptance of the Christian virtues of humility, tolerance, and charity. That latter-day Christian romanticism explains White's reliance on sentiment in his fiction, his emphasis on character in his magazine sketches, and his appeal to a reader's senses of compassion and humor in his editorials. But unlike Emerson, and Jesus too perhaps, White was constitutionally unable to accept with serenity a slow, nearly timeless pace of progress, a pace measured in millenia. He was, like his hero Teddy Roosevelt, a man of spontaneous action who worked not only to marshal public opinion but to apply it as well. Thus he became a Kansas political boss with national influence, a highly visible backstage politician who fought vigorously and skillfully for legislated social change during much of his life. That duality in his life and career of the ideal and the practical is demonstrated well in a definition of democracy he wrote late in life for *Scholastic Magazine*: "Democracy is the institutionalized expression of the Christian philosophy in ordinary life," at base "an attitude of mind."[3]

In 1927 Elizabeth Sergeant in a sketch of White for *Century Magazine* remarked that he approached life with the mission of a moralist and the gusto of a boxer, then repeated what TR once said of him: "He preaches what he practices."[4] That matrix of zeal and zest formed but also limited his career as a writer. For in his writings, especially his fiction, he reiterates didactically the thesis that the spiritual, not the material is of true importance, until he reminds us of a one-stringed fiddle player practicing variations adeptly but monotonously on the one motif that "the divine spark is in every soul" and "is the realest thing we know in the universe."[5] Thus Francis

Hackett exclaimed with some exasperation in a review of *In the Heart of a Fool*, "Well, William Allen White . . . you are an artist. When you are not an ambassador or an editor or a reporter or a publicity man or a Progressive, you are an artist—sometimes, even, when you are one or all of these."[6] Similarly, he curtailed the potential appeal of his nonfiction magazine contributions by an immediate topicality. In them he usually addressed serious issues, but they were issues of the day for the day. Russell Blankenship in his history of American literature placed a high value on *The Old Order Changeth* but did so precisely because of its topical, representative nature: "This little book sets forth the political and social creed of those moderates who formed the center of the Progressive party in 1912. As a political guide for to-day, it is as archaic as a platform of the Know-Nothing party, but it gives the student an excellent idea of principles that were widely accepted during the first twelve or fifteen years of the present century."[7]

In 1938, in answer to criticism that he had dissipated his imaginative talent as a writer of fiction in the ephemera of journalism and politics, White wrote: "If I had devoted my life to writing I would probably have been about where Booth Tarkington is now—maybe! Well, at that, I think I have had as much fun as Booth Tarkington. I think I will leave about as much of my personality in the history and institutions of my country as Booth. . . . I don't regret that I came out of the cloister and have lived my life in my own way."[8] In living that life he expressed his belief in man's "divine spark," supporting the twin causes of individual liberty and political reform with native pragmatism. He played the game of politics to impress upon it his convictions, but he played it in his own way, with verve and optimism, as exemplified in his hyperbolic description of his working relationship with TR: "a gay and festive friendship of two middle aged men gently tossing dynamite about in a dazed and astounded world."[9] In pursuing his duality of purpose and practice from the editor's desk of the *Emporia Gazette*, White achieved, paradoxically, a lasting place in our national archives as a provincial but representative publicist for the progressive spirit. And that is White's value for today: in his life and works he combined the roles of moralist and activist with that of publicist for over forty years, fully half of them after the end of the Progressive Movement itself. Hence the editors of the standard *Literary History of the United States*, in assessing the reform sentiment of that era, assert that "there is no more representative figure in this whole period than William Allen White, of Emporia, Kansas."[10]

For White, following his duality of purpose and practice, was well within the amorphous philosophical mainstream of the Progressive Movement, with its cross currents of idealism and pragmatism, of social Christianity and "social engineering." But he was not within the mainstream traditions of Midwest insurgency, as pointed out by the social historian Russel Nye. In *Midwestern Progressive Politics* Nye observed that White "was never a true Midwestern progressive," that he was too genteel to "have in him the hell-for-leather heritage of Midwest independency." Instead, Nye suggested, his was "the progressivism of Theodore Roosevelt and the Easterners, upper middle-class liberalism rather than Granger-Populist 'radicalism.' "[11] Quite true, White never did identify with the class protest implicit in the rural and, to a much lesser degree, labor-dominated People's party. But that does not mean he was not a representative Midwestern progressive. He spoke for small-town, not rural or industrialized Mid-America. He was a Rotarian, not a Granger—a Congregationalist, not a Baptist—an employer who had to meet a payroll, not an employee collecting a paycheck. By heritage he was a member of the solidly middle-class power structure of his state. By choice he became a leader of the liberal wing of its Republican party. As such, his brand of progressivism was as indigenous to the Midwest as that of the more radical Bob La Follette of Wisconsin. The "Easterners" White relied on most for theoretical and moral support, as he moved at the turn of the century to a position of moderate liberalism, were the staff of *McClure's*. In describing that group, Justin Kaplan, the biographer of Lincoln Steffens, observed: "McClure and his writers, in an era when the average American did not go beyond the fifth grade in school, had all gone to college, but the colleges they went to— Knox, Allegheny, Michigan State, Berkeley—were remote from the East in spirit as well as in place."[12] Those journalists were all of the same generation and had experienced similarly the depression years of the early 1890s. Among them, according to Kaplan, "what passed for a common body of theory and belief was a cracker-barrel mixture of the meliorism, service ethic, and Christian principles of the social gospel and values of the Republic traditionally attributed to the Founding Fathers. One could also detect traces of Abolitionist Fervor, populist outrage, recollections of the Haymarket Square riots in Chicago, Homestead, Pullman, the Panic and Coxey's Army."[13]

White's liberalism was firmly rooted in such Midwestern "thought," his identity cognate with Midwestern small-town "gentry."

Nye also declares that White's greatest contribution as a publicist came after the progressive era, because he kept progressive ideals alive in the Republican party through the feverish war years and the cynical twenties: "In the 'back to normalcy' period of Will Hays and Harding, White was a constant nagging reminder to the Republican satrapy of the liberal tradition of earlier days."[14] But social historian Kenneth S. Davis reports that in the 1930s many liberals came to believe otherwise, that they "saw not the slightest evidence that White had a liberalizing influence upon the Republican party. Instead, they saw abundant evidence of the value to the GOP of what they deemed his sophistry—his talent for making the dull seem interesting, for cloaking with sympathetic attractiveness what was nakedly repulsive, for (in general) making the worse seem the better cause."[15] Both observations embrace that greased pig Truth. In the 1920s White returned to the Republican party to cry out in its "wilderness" with a vigorous and independent voice, while endorsing the national tickets and occasionally commending the subsequent administrations, even Harding's. But in the 1930s, for whatever personal reasons—age, loyalty, habit, political friendships and obligations, a commitment to state reform programs—he put his ties to the moderate wing of the Kansas Republican party above larger considerations and helped whitewash what most former progressives regarded, on the national level at least, as a hopelessly begrimed sepulcher, the old-line Republican party. For he opposed the elections of FDR while warmly supporting most of his New Deal measures and his prewar and wartime foreign policies. Yet in that Will was no sinister hypocrite, though he has seemed so to Kenneth Davis and others. White was sometimes confused, inconsistent, even equivocal, but he was never consciously cynical: his oft-repeated excuse was that as a moderate liberal he could do more practical good inside the dominant party of his state (and, during much of his life, the nation) than out. At the close of his life, from the perspective of the late 1930s, he himself was not so sure of the validity of that excuse, though he continued, rather schizophrenically, his much-tempered allegiance to the Republican party. As he explained humbly in 1938 in a letter to the young radical Gil Wilson: "I have probably done as much to convince the world of the injustices of our economic system as if I had moved further left and limited my audience and my appeal, but I am not sure even about that. It is a guess and maybe I am just salving my conscience. ..."[16]

Regardless of our views about White's ultimate effect on American politics, we must acknowledge that he was a remarkably effective political publicist. Perhaps the best example of that came near the end of his life when he led the successful effort to lobby Congress to support critically needed aid to the beleaguered Allies. Edward Lord Halifax, British ambassador to the United States during the war, immediately sent a telegram of condolence to Sallie when Will died, affirming that "the cause of Anglo-American co-operation owes an unpayable debt to him for his generous and unsparing efforts to bring a better understanding between our peoples. ..."[17] White's efforts as a publicist were effective because he was a likable "character," an eminently quotable humorist and stylist, an independent editor who viewed events and commented about them with blithe singularity. And he was effective because he spoke to and for a large constituency who regarded him an exemplar of familiar country-town virtues and commonsense liberalism. He was an outland prophet preaching the moral imperative of "old-fashioned" universal brotherhood to a materialistic, unrighteous people. And like the prophets of old he preached through words and deeds. In a tribute to White in the *Saturday Review* Henry S. Canby wrote: "One saw in him how a good molder of public opinion functions. He must have honesty himself, he must have modesty, he must have courage, he must have deep convictions, he must (whether in books or in life) be willing to believe that his opponent is as human as himself."[18] In all his efforts to turn private into public opinion he exuded a warmhearted vitality and joy that captivated conservative and radical alike. In his pragmatic promotion of a Christian transcendentalism—in his gusto, humor, and shrewd simplicity—William Allen White was the public voice of Middlewestern middle-class American democracy for two generations.

Notes and References

Chapter One

1. Many of the details of White's early life, and their interpretations, either here or in the several biographies, are necessarily gathered from his various autobiographical commentaries.

2. Vernon L. Parrington, *Main Currents in American Thought: An Interpretation of American Literature from the Beginnings to 1920* (New York: Harcourt, Brace, 1930), 3:374.

3. William Allen White, *Forty Years on Main Street*, ed. Russell H. Fitzgibbon (New York, 1937), p. 6.

4. *The Autobiography of William Allen White* (New York, 1946), p. 145.

5. Ibid., p. 175.

6. Everett Rich in *William Allen White, the Man from Emporia* (New York, 1941) asserts that White's "twenty-one months under Bent Murdock were one of the most profitable periods of his life" (p. 56).

7. In a letter of 28 July 1921 to his publisher George Brett, president of Macmillan Company, White wrote, "as you know her [Mrs. White's] judgment is keen and wise, and I never submit a manuscript of any importance until we have gone over it line upon line and precept upon precept (White Collection, Library of Congress). W. L. White in "The Sage of Emporia" (*Nieman Reports* 23 [March 1969]:25), observed, "In a way she was less stable than my father; she had ups and downs. She would be sparkling and gay, and then could follow periods of depression. In another way she was more stable. She had hard common sense, and a deep sense of fairness. She also had, herself, some talent for writing, and shrewd literary judgment.... He never wrote a piece of any importance without their going over it together."

8. White, *Forty Years*, pp. 4–6.

9. For a circumstantial history of Lyon County newspapers, including financial details of White's purchase of the *Gazette*, see Laura M. French, *History of Emporia and Lyon County* (Emporia: Emporia Gazette Print, 1929), pp. 222–29.

10. In his autobiography (279) White remembers his immediate reason for going to Colorado and Sallie that weekend was these proofs, but he did not sign the contract for *The Real Issue* until the last of August. The extrinsic notation 8/15 on an undated letter he sent to W. I. Way urging that publisher to make a definitive offer suggests that White's

memory after nearly fifty years blended these events (White Collection, Emporia State University).

11. William Allen White, "Thirty Years Ago," *Emporia Weekly Gazette*, 19 August 1926, p. 1.

12. White, *Forty Years*, p. 270.

13. White's home at 927 Exchange Street became an oasis for many of his out-of-state friends on their ways cross country. For example, his close friend novelist Edna Ferber in her autobiography, *A Peculiar Treasure* (New York: Doubleday, Doran, 1939), wrote: "When your world is awry and hope dead and vitality low and the appetite gone there is no ocean trip, no month in the country, no known drug equal to the reviving quality of twenty-four hours spent on the front porch or in the sitting room of the Whites' house in Emporia" (p. 227).

14. William Allen White, "Howells in Emporia," *Emporia Weekly Gazette*, 11 March 1937, p. 1.

15. William Allen White, "Over Trails of Gold, The Story of a Visit During the Past Summer to the Big Creek Camp, In Idaho's Thunder Mountain Mining District, and What It Disclosed," *United States Mining Journal* 2 (December 1903):1–7; "Over Trails of Gold, In the Treasure Hills of Thunder Mountain," ibid., 3 (April 1904):1–5.

16. *Mark Twain's Letters*, ed. Albert Bigelow Paine (New York: Harper & Brothers, 1917), 2:797.

17. Quoted by Walter Johnson in *William Allen White's America* (New York, 1947), p. 160.

18. The *Collier's* article—"Long of Kansas," 18 July 1908, pp. 8–9, 22—was by-lined "J. M. Oskison." Robert S. La Forte suggests in *Leaders of Reform* (Lawrence, 1974), p. 105, that White himself wrote the article; certainly everything within it points to him.

19. In May 1912 White published his by–then quite partisan version of these events in the *American Magazine* as "Should Old Acquaintance Be Forgot: A Statement of the Relations Between President Taft and His Friend Colonel Roosevelt" (13–18), which caused John S. Phillips to remark in a note after the article: "The editor of The American Magazine, though realizing how close Mr. White is to Colonel Roosevelt, finds it impossible to follow his friend and collaborator in all his interpretations of personal fact."

20. For a discussion of White's contribution to that speech see Robert S. La Forte, "Theodore Roosevelt's Osawatomie Speech," *Kansas Historical Quarterly* 32 (Summer 1966):191–92.

Chapter Two

1. Quoted by Johnson, p. 265.

2. White Collection, Library of Congress. Typically, White expressed

the same sentiment in a *Gazette* editorial at this time: "It's vastly wiser to put on your best clothes and usher at your old girl's wedding than to rock the house or shoot at the groom" (Emporia *Weekly Gazette,* 9 September 1920, p. 1).

3. *Selected Letters of William Allen White, 1899–1943,* ed. Walter Johnson (New York, 1947), p. 213; letter dated 8 December 1920.

4. Letter dated 28 May 1921, White Collection, Library of Congress. Lorimer assigned him a "farmer story" which appeared as the article "Farmer John and the Sirens," 12 November 1921, pp. 10–11, 53–54. Sallie was deeply depressed by her daughter's death and did not become reconciled to that loss for years.

5. Such an output seems extraordinary when we remember his other commitments, but whenever possible White made his work do double duty all his life. For example, in the *New York Herald Tribune Magazine* of Sunday, 23 August 1922, pp. 8–9, his "As I See It" commentary consisted of six separate observations; several were reprinted as editorials in the *Gazette* the following week. Apparently unaware of this practice, Helen Mahin included one, "Why We Never Die," in her collection of his *Gazette* editorials, *The Editor and His People* (New York, 1924), p. 175, and ascribed it to the Tuesday issue, 25 August 1922.

6. Letter to Knox, 3 July 1934, White Collection, Library of Congress.

7. Letter dated 15 July 1926, White Collection, Library of Congress.

8. As quoted by Anne O'Hare McCormick, who covered one of his speeches at Harrington, Kansas, for a full-page by-lined feature, "Editor White Tilts at the Kansas Klan," in the *New York Times,* 5 October, sec. 9, p. 1.

9. In "The Sage of Emporia" White's son viewed that campaign as a local disaster: "The morning after election, the Eastern Seaboard press was hailing William Allen White for having swept the Klan from Kansas. Back home we had another view. In his race for Governor, he had run third. We had a Klan-endorsed Mayor, and had elected a Klan-endorsed sheriff. And my father had lost his own county—the deepest humiliation a politician can have.... [So] regardless of the glowing editorials written by liberals across the land, we in the family knew that it had been a bone-crunching defeat, that in the State, the County and the City, all had been lost save honor and that, as practical politicians, it would take us several years of hard work to pick up the pieces of this Noble Victory and stick them together again" (pp. 26–27).

10. White, *Selected Letters,* p. 250; letter of W. S. Fitzpatrick, 24 November 1925.

11. Quoted by Johnson, p. 399.

12. William Allen White, "The Education of Herbert Hoover," 9 June 1928, pp. 8–9, 42–44.

13. William Allen White, "Editorial Correspondence," *Emporia Weekly Gazette*, 14 June 1928, p. 1.

14. Letter to William Borah, 6 May 1927, White Collection, Library of Congress.

15. Letter to James Kerney, editor of *Trenton Times*, 5 December 1930, White Collection, Library of Congress.

16. Quoted by Johnson, p. 436.

17. Letter to Harold Ickes, 14 July 1932, White Collection, Library of Congress.

18. White, *Selected Letters*, p. 335.

19. White, *Forty Years*, p. 213.

20. White's son wrote a thinly disguised novel about those events, *What People Said* (New York: Viking Press, 1938), which is of interest not only because it explores the relationship of the two families but also because in it he viewed his father with mildly resentful subservience. He had worked on the *Gazette* from ca. 1924 to 1934, then left Emporia for the East Coast to build his own eventually successful career as a journalist and war correspondent, publishing a total of thirteen books of his own; one, *They Were Expendable*, was a war-time best-seller. For a thorough, scholarly treatment of the Finney scandal see Robert S. Bader, *The Great Kansas Bond Scandal* (Lawrence, Kans., 1982).

21. Letter dated 29 February 1936, White Collection, Library of Congress.

22. "William Allen White of Emporia: An American Institution is Seventy," *Life*, 28 February 1938, pp. 9–13; "William Allen White: The Sage of Emporia," *Look*, 15 February 1938, pp. 9–11.

23. David Hinshaw, *A Man from Kansas: The Story of William Allen White* (New York, 1945), p. 177.

24. *F. D. R. His Personal Letters 1928–1945*, ed. Elliott Roosevelt (New York: Duell, Sloan and Pearce, 1950), 2:968.

25. William Allen White, "The Answer to Prayer?" *Emporia Weekly Gazette*, 11 December 1941, p. 1.

26. Letter dated 21 July 1941, White Collection, Library of Congress.

27. William Allen White, "Home Again, Jiggity-Jig," *Emporia Weekly Gazette*, 4 February 1943, p. 1.

28. Quoted by Johnson, p. 570, from *Philadelphia Record*, 31 August 1943.

29. Telegram dated 29 January 1944, White Collection, Emporia State University.

Chapter Three

1. Oswald G. Villard, *Some Newspapers and Newspaper-Men* (New York: Alfred A. Knopf, 1923), p. 244.

2. Quoted by W. A. Swanberg, *Pulitzer* (New York: Charles Scribner's Sons, 1967), p. 403.

3. McCormick, *New York Times*, 5 October 1924, sec. 9, p. 1.

4. "The *Gazette*'s Bicentennial Album," *Emporia Gazette*, 24 January 1976, p. 2.

5. White, *Forty Years*, p. 32.

6. White, *Autobiography*, p. 626.

7. William Allen White, "How Free Is the Press?" *Collier's*, 8 April 1939, p. 88.

8. White, *Forty Years*, p. 251.

9. Letter to Will T. Beck, 23 February 1942; quoted by Johnson, p. 559.

10. In his *Atlantic Monthly* article "Good Newspapers and Bad" White wrote with reference to Fred G. Bonfils and Harry H. Tammen of the Denver *Post*, "They and their kind represent today the only sort of journalism that the newly literate moron in American life can understand and enjoy. This moron's name is legion" (153 [May 1934]:584).

11. 9 April 1900, White Collection, Library of Congress. White's contempt for yellow journalism was lifelong and consistent. In a letter answering a protest from Guy T. Viskniskki of Republic Syndicate White wrote, "Hearst is my idea of a rattlesnake crossed with smallpox. I do not like him or any of his works, and I would not work for him for any money on earth" (9 September 1921, White Collection, Library of Congress).

12. William Allen White, "The Man Who Made the 'Star,'" *Collier's*, 26 June 1915, p. 13.

13. William Allen White, "The Ethics of Advertising," *Atlantic Monthly*, 164 (November 1939):665–66.

14. In the "Style Book for Proof-Readers, Reporters and Printers of the Emporia *Gazette*," compiled by city editor Laura French, one rule reads: "Don't use Mr. White's name—say Gazette, or cut it out altogether if you can't say Gazette. You might lose your job otherwise" (2d ed., 1 March 1919, p. 3; copy in Spencer Research Library, University of Kansas).

15. White, *Forty Years*, p. 274.

16. In a letter to Charles Driscoll of the McNaught Syndicate 29 July 1939 White explained his relationship with Mason, who in temperament and political philosophy was so different from him, in a figure of speech that helps explain his many diverse friendships: "Walt and I never had much real converse. We got to know each other like two horses in the corner of a pasture standing end to end and each with his neck over the other's back switching flies. In that way an affection grew that needed no words and never had the slightest vocal expression" (Spencer Research Library, University of Kansas). His use of that trope also helps

explain why his writing style remained sprightly despite a voluminous output over more than a half-century: he seldom forgot a catchy comparison or phrase and did not shrink from recycling it. For instance, in his 1925 biography of Calvin Coolidge he describes the growth of a friendship between the taciturn Coolidge and the Boston retailer and publicist Frank Stearns: "The two must have sat many silent hours smoking, like two horses cross-necked in the corner of a pasture, getting acquainted without words!" (p. 73). In the 1938 biography he reworks the image nearer to that in the 1939 letter: "Two farm horses in a fence corner—haunch to neck—flapping flies with their tails, must have the same spiritual satisfaction that gave those two men their sparse delight" (p. 141).

17. "The Gazette's Bicentennial Album," *Emporia Gazette*, 7 February 1976, p. 1.

18. Allan Nevins, *American Press Opinion* (New York: D. C. Heath and Co., 1928), p. v.

19. In a letter to a Mrs. Minnie Moody 25 January 1938 White wrote that *Forty Years on Main Street* "wasn't my book. I receive no royalties from it. It was compiled by a young college professor who came to the Gazette office. I wrote a few footnotes for him" (Spencer Research Library, University of Kansas). In the book White commented in a note to one of the sections: "This is a good place to remark that some of the editorials in this book I did not write. I have a lingering suspicion that three or four in this group were handed in by young men and women working on *The Gazette*. They flattered me most sincerely by trying to imitate me and in reading their copy I helped them by adding a phrase here, a sentence there, a paragraph perhaps at the end" (pp. 373–74). Walter Johnson observed in a footnote to his biography that "some of the editorials in this volume attributed to W. A. White were actually written by W. L. White" (p. 602). In "The Sage of Emporia" W. L. remarked that "a few years after I left Emporia [my father] mailed me a book gotten up by some scholar who had come to Emporia to make a compilation of Gazette editorials. With the book was a note, saying that he rather thought that some of the editorials in it had been written by me. Reading through it, I found that, in the period when I had been actively on the editorial page, about two thirds of those editorials picked by this scholar as The Gazette's best actually had been written by me" (p. 27). Those several remarks do pose for us a problem of textual authenticity whenever we use that collection. For this study, therefore, I have made sure that any editorial cited from that volume and dated from 1925 through 1934 was indeed written by W. A. White. I thank Mrs. Kathrine (W. L.) White for calling my attention to this problem.

20. White, *Forty Years*, pp. 276–77.

21. Oswald G. Villard, review of *Forty Years on Main Street* in *Nation*, 24 April 1937, p. 476.

22. White, *The Edit~r*, p. 303.

23. Ibid., p. 254.

24. White, *Forty Years*, pp. 199–200.

25. Ibid., p. 191.

26. White, *The Editor*, p. 141.

27. White, *Forty Years*, p. 366.

28. Hinshaw, *A Man from Kansas*, p. 89.

29. Frank Clough, *William Allen White of Emporia* (New York, 1941), p. 5.

30. White, *The Editor*, p. 98.

31. *Emporia Gazette*, 18 February 1899, p. 2.

32. White, *Forty Years*, p. 19.

33. White, *The Editor*, p. 231.

34. Ibid., pp. 232–33.

35. Ibid., pp. 30–31.

36. Quoted by Elmer Ellis, *Mr. Dooley's America: A Life of Finley Peter Dunne* (New York: Alfred A. Knopf, 1941), p. 216.

37. William Allen White, *Masks in a Pageant* (New York, 1928), p. vii.

38. The articles White did not alter substantially are "Croker," *McClure's* 16 (February 1901):317–26; "Platt," *McClure's* 18 (December 1901):145–53; "Harrison," *Cosmopolitan* 32 (March 1902):489–96; "Cleveland," *McClure's* 18 (February 1902):322–30; "Hanna," *McClure's* 16 (November 1900):56–64; "Al Smith, City Feller," *Collier's*, 21 August 1926, pp. 8–9, 42–43; and "They Can't Beat My Big Boy," *Collier's*, 18 June 1927, pp. 8–9, 45–47. The ones he rewrote extensively or added significantly more material to are "McKinley and Hanna," *Saturday Evening Post*, 12 March 1904, pp. 1–2; "Bryan," *McClure's* 15 (July 1900):232–37; "Theodore Roosevelt," *McClure's* 18 (November 1901): 40–47; "Taft, a Hewer of Wood," *American Magazine* 66 (May 1908): 19–32; "Common Man on Uncommon Job," New York *Herald Tribune Magazine*, 4 March 1923, pp. 5–6. The Coolidge and Wilson chapters also use material from articles connected with the two biographies in book form.

39. White, "Bryan," p. 232.

40. White, "Cleveland," p. 329.

41. White, "Croker," p. 324; p. 22 in book version.

42. White, "Al Smith," p. 8; p. 475 in book version.

43. White, "Hanna," p. 56.

44. White, "Platt," p. 148; p. 44 in book version.

45. White, "Croker," p. 319; p. 3 in book version.

46. In "Progressivism and the Masculinity Crisis," *Psychological Review* 61 (Fall 1974):443–55, Joe L. Dubbert suggests White believed himself threatened by "an effeminate society and culture" and was propelled by feelings of sexual insecurity to seek leaders of power, dominance, and masculinity. That thesis is interesting but not well substantiated in the article. White was a hearty extrovert who admired courage, energy, and bluffness; if he subconsciously reacted against "passive" feminine aggression in his choice of heroes, he certainly hid it well behind a strong advocacy of women's rights. On the other hand, as a Christian sentimentalist, he did preach the beatitudes at every opportunity, which to a psychoanalytic critic may reveal an even more fundamental effeminism.

47. White, "Bryan," p. 235. By the light of twenty-eight later years White revised one of the sentences of this passage to read, "He was more than three-fourths brave, which a demagogue is not" (p. 253).

48. The six articles correlate to the chapters thus: chapter 2, vol. 67, January 1909; chapter 3, February 1909; chapter 4, March 1909; chapter 5, April 1909; chapter 6, vol. 68, May 1909; chapter 7, August 1909; and chapter 8, vol. 69, February 1910.

49. Apparently, he or Sallie was proud of his 1908 coverage, for one of them, or a secretary, put together a scrapbook containing his syndicated material as furnished by a clipping service plus much press commentary both complimentary and critical; it is housed at the Spencer Research Library, University of Kansas. Likewise, in the 1920s someone compiled scrapbooks containing his *Judge* and *New York Herald Tribune* material, together with many of his other magazine and newspaper contributions at that time; those are in the White Collection, Emporia State University.

50. Cited by Jean L. Kennedy in "William Allen White: A Study of the Interrelationship of Press, Power and Party Politics" (Ph.D. diss., University of Kansas, 1981), p. 176. Of the five doctoral dissertations about White that I have read, this one, focused on his career from 1896–1916, seems the most thorough.

51. Letter of 5 December 1917, White Collection, Library of Congress.

52. Edwin Emory, *The Press and America: An Interpretative History of the Mass Media* (Englewood Cliffs, N.J.: Prentice-Hall, 1978), p. 311.

53. Elmo S. Watson, *A History of Newspaper Syndicates in the United States, 1865–1935* (Chicago: Publisher's Auxiliary, 1936), p. 39.

54. William Allen White Sizes 'Em Up," *Colliers*, 9 August 1924, pp. 7–8, 27.

55. William Allen White, "The Casting Out of Jimmy Myers," *Saturday Evening Post*, 23 December 1905, p. 4.

56. William Allen White, "40 Years: New Men, Old Issues," *New York Times Magazine*, 9 August 1936, pp. 1–2, 15; and "Landon: I

Knew Him When," *Saturday Evening Post*, 18 July 1936, pp. 5–7, 68, 70, 72–73.

Chapter Four

1. *New York Times*, 12 June 1901, p. 380.
2. Richard Hofstadter, "Winston Churchill: A Study in the Popular Novel," *American Quarterly*, 2 (Spring 1950), 13.
3. Charles C. Baldwin, *The Men Who Make Our Novels* (New York: Dodd, Mead, 1925), p. 559.
4. William Allen White, "The Other Side of Main Street," *Collier's*, 30 July 1921, p. 18.
5. Burton Roscoe, "Contemporary Reminiscences," *Arts and Decorations* 30 (November 1928):100.
6. *Dial*, 1 January 1897, p. 24.
7. White remarked in the *Autobiography*, "My favorite story of all . . . Bible stories was the story of the prodigal son. . . . I suppose unconsciously that was the story of my own inner life" (373).
8. They appeared together in *McClure's* 8 (February 1897):321–30.
9. Cf., Brander Matthews, "Her Letter to His Second Wife," *Cosmopolitan* 25 (May 1898):56–64.
10. White, "The Other Side of Main Street," p. 7.
11. Undoubtedly, White lifted the name "Heart's Desire" from Psalm 10:3, "For the wicked boasteth of his heart's desire . . . ," an example of the many offhand biblical allusions that lace his prose and mark his style.
12. Robert Bridges ["Droch"], review in *Life*, 7 January 1897, p. 7.
13. Cited by Johnson, p. 115, with reference to an account in the *Kansas City World* 29 December 1899.
14. William Allen White, "Boys Then and Now," *American Magazine*, March 1926, pp. 7–9, 112, 115–16.
15. Mark Van Doren, *Contemporary American Novelists 1900–1920* (New York: Macmillan Co., 1922), p. 136.
16. H. L. Mencken, "The Last of the Victorians," *Smart Set* 29 (October 1909):154.
17. Robert Van Gelder, "Spring Books," *New York Times Book Review*, 26 March 1944, p. 1.
18. W. D. Howells, "Psychological Counter-Current in Recent Fiction," *North American Review* 173 (December 1901):877.
19. White had Simpson specifically in mind when he planned this story. In a letter of 21 November 1899 to Thomas W. Johnston, managing editor of the *Kansas City Star*, he wrote: "In 1894, when Jerry Simpson was sick and about to die, I took two days off from my work on the

"Star," and wrote a biography of him. I put [*sic*] a good deal of local color, and a somewhat extended description of the Alliance movement in Kansas. The whole story was in the 'morgue' when I left, and Rich told me it was there not long ago. Just now I am engaged on a story for the Scribner, in which I want to put considerable of the Alliance Movement, that I described at considerable length in that story of Simpson. I wish you would lend me for a few days that story, if it is still in the morgue, and I will return it when I have read it over and refreshed my memory on certain points...." (White Collection, Library of Congress). Robert Bridges, editor of *Scribner's*, declined the story, so White revamped it and placed it with the *Saturday Evening Post*; Scribner's then included it in the collection.

20. Compare pp. 315–20 to "Something about Your Pa," *Gazette*, 21 January 1904 (*The Editor*, pp. 107–10) or compare pp. 332–35 to "The Meeting Place," *Gazette*, 5 February 1903 (*Forty Years*, pp. 354–56).

21. Eskridge, who was one of Emporia's original settlers, committed suicide November 1900 because of financial losses caused by the 1898 failure of the town's First National Bank, according to Laura M. French in her *History of Emporia and Lyon County*, p. 71. She did not mention in her history that by 1900 the *Republican* had lost much of its circulation, advertising, and political patronage to the *Gazette*; thus this story must have pained many Emporians by its uncharitable local allusiveness.

22. "Saturday Review of Books," *New York Times*, 14 July 1906, p. 45.

23. Johnson, p. 152.

24. *The Outlook*, 21 August 1909, p. 922.

25. *New York Times*, 31 July 1909, p. 462.

26. H. L. Mencken, *Smart Set*, pp. 153–55.

27. John D. McKee, *William Allen White: Maverick on Main Street* (Westport, Conn.: 1975), p. 131.

28. Letter 31 March 1916 as quoted by Johnson, p. 258.

29. Parrington, *Main Currents*, 3:348.

30. *Springfield Republican*, 3 September 1916, p. 15.

31. Letters dated 24 August 1917 to George Brett and August F. Jaccacci mention this book project. White Collection, Emporia State University.

32. Rich, *William Allen White, the Man from Emporia*, p. 200. At the time the Whites too believed the public mood was inauspicious; in a letter of 27 May 1918 to George Brett, Will wrote: "Mrs. White and I are in grave doubt about publishing the novel at this time. We feel that the public is not interested in fiction. Possibly the losses of the war may turn their minds away from the war but so far they are engrossed in war books. I feel that the novel would fall flat, that it would not have the

audience which seven years of work on it has fairly earned for it" (White Collection, Library of Congress).

33. Francis Hackett, review "In the Heart of a Fool," *New Republic*, 15 February 1919, p. 91.

34. William Allen White, "Splitting Fiction Three Ways," *New Republic*, 12 April 1922, p. 23.

35. *H. L. Mencken's "Smart Set" Criticism*, ed. William H. Nolte (Ithaca: Cornell University Press, 1968), p. 265.

36. William Allen White, "Movie People Distorted My Book, *In the Heart of a Fool*," *New York Times*, 24 February 1921, p. 16; earlier *A Certain Rich Man* had also been made into a movie. During evening prime-time, 18 November 1977, the ABC Television Network featured a made-for-television movie based on the Mary White editorial; the IBM corporation sponsored that showing and announced it in full-page ads placed in major newspapers country-wide, which reprinted White's piece in total. Will should have approved of that production, had he been alive. See Caryl Ledner's *Mary White* (New York, 1977) for that filmscript issued as a "promotional novel."

37. Letter dated 29 April 1921, White Collection, Library of Congress.

Chapter Five

1. White, *Selected Letters*, p. 212.

2. William Allen White, "Are Human Movements Independent of Wars?" *Journal of Social Forces* 3 (May 1925):593-95; "The Larger Cycle of American Development," ibid., 4 (September 1925):1-5; "An Earlier Cycle of American Development," ibid., 4 (December 1925):181-85.

3. Letter dated 5 December 1939, White Collection, Library of Congress. In this letter White misremembered the second article connected with his book, the articles used are actually "The Farmer's Votes and Problems," *Yale Review* 28 (March 1939):443-48, and "How May the West Survive?" *North American Review* 248 (Autumn 1939):7-17.

4. White, *Forty Years*, p. 244.

5. White, *Selected Letters*, p. 252.

6. In a letter of 2 October 1919 to George Brett, White wrote: "Houghton Mifflin Company are getting out a Modern American Statesman Series and they want me to do Wilson. I don't want to break the chain of my luck, and I don't want to publish my books away from Macmillans. Can you suggest any way I can do this thing and let you hold the copyright and publish the book outside the series, and still keep the thing in the series?" (White Collection, Library of Congress).

7. Claude G. Bowers, review of *Woodrow Wilson* in *New York World*, 23 November 1924, p. 9.

8. Edward H. O'Neill, *A History of American Biography* (Philadelphia: University of Pennsylvania Press, 1935), p. 336.

9. White, *Selected Letters*, p. 252.

10. *Review of Reviews* 73 (January 1926):110.

11. Donald R. McCoy, *Calvin Coolidge: the Quiet President* (New York: Macmillan, Co., 1967), p. 425.

12. As quoted by Johnson, p. 474.

13. Silver, "Coolidge and the Historians," *American Scholar* 50 (Autumn 1981), 508–9.

14. Will Irwin, review of *The Autobiography* in *Saturday Review of Literature*, 16 March 1946, p. 7.

15. White, *A Puritan in Babylon*, p. 42.

16. Charles Eskridge in the *Republican*, 4 June 1895, p. 2.

17. *A Memorial to a Great American*, comp. Everett Rich, 2d ed. (Emporia: Teachers College Press, n.d.), p. [13].

18. La Forte, *Leaders*, pp. 253–54; Garraty, *Right-Hand Man, the Life of George W. Perkins* (New York: Harper & Brothers, 1960), p. 340.

19. In September he started out dubious to be sure, writing "Neither party is God's perfect child. Both have glaring faults. No one should pretend that a perfectly ideal condition exists in either party, nor one which satisfies the yearnings of any normal heart attuned to song of the morning stars. Yet life's decisions, which always are made with qualifications and restrictions, are, after all, made in the rough, and bulking the matter largely, it would seem wise to advise Republicans to vote their ticket this year" (*Emporia Weekly Gazette*, 9 September 1920, p. 1). But by October he was writing "Harding entered [the campaign] without distinction; he is going out a fair-minded, dignified, earnest, sincerely honest American gentleman" (7 October 1920, p. 1).

20. Letter dated 23 May 1903 (misdated 1905), White Collection, Library of Congress.

21. Letter dated 12 January 1906, White Collection, Library of Congress.

Chapter Six

1. White, *Forty Years*, p. 5.

2. William Allen White, *A Theory of Spiritual Progress* (Emporia, 1910), pp. 11–12.

3. "What Democracy Means to Me," *Scholastic Magazine*, 23 October 1937, p. 9.

4. Elizabeth Sergeant, "The Citizen from Emporia," *Century Magazine*, January 1927, p. 309.

5. White, *A Theory of Spiritual Progress*, pp. 50, 52.

6. Hackett, *New Republic*, 15 February 1919, p. 91.

7. Russell Blankenship, *American Literature* (New York: Holt, Rinehart and Winston, 1958), p. 652.

8. Letter to Charles M. Harger, 7 February 1938, as quoted by Johnson, p. 153.

9. Letter to George Brett, 13 November 1919, White Collection, Library of Congress.

10. Robert E. Spiller, Willard Thorp et al. *Literary History of the United States* (New York: Macmillan, 1963), p. 1117.

11. Russel Nye, *Midwestern Progressive Politics: a Historical Study of Its Origins and Development 1870–1950* (East Lansing: Michigan State University Press, 1951), p. 237.

12. Justin Kaplan, *Lincoln Steffens: a Biography* (New York: Simon and Schuster, 1974), p. 117.

13. Ibid., p. 120.

14. Nye, p. 237.

15. "The Sage of Emporia," *American Heritage* 30 (October–November 1979):93.

16. *Letters of William Allen White and a Young Man*, ed. Gil Wilson (New York, 1948), p. 76.

17. Dated 29 January 1944, White Collection, Emporia State University.

18. Henry S. Canby, "A Personal Tribute," *Saturday Review*, 5 February 1944, p. 16.

Selected Bibliography

PRIMARY SOURCES

1. Bibliographies

Walter Johnson and Alberta Pantle have compiled "A Bibliography of the Published Works of William Allen White" (*Kansas Historical Quarterly* 15 [February 1947]:22–41); it includes his books, most of his substantive magazine articles, and a few interpretive book reviews and special newspaper features. No one has attempted a listing of his everyday or his syndicated journalism, but Donald Pady has compiled "A Bibliography of the Poems of William Allen White" (*Bulletin of Bibliography* 25 [January–April 1967]: 44–46). The papers of William Allen White at the Library of Congress are well catalogued; that collection includes eighty letterbooks chronologically arranged and separately indexed, 429 containers of general correspondence arranged in alphabetical order by years with a general index, and twenty-seven containers of miscellany. See "Registers of Papers in the Manuscript Division of the Library of Congress," no. 52 (1978). All manuscript materials and published articles in the White Collection at Emporia State University are indexed in *A Bibliography of William Allen White*, 2 vols. (Emporia: Teachers College Press, 1969). Because these several bibliographies are readily available, only White's writings published in book format are listed below.

2. Fiction

A Certain Rich Man. New York: Macmillan Co., 1909.
The Court of Boyville. New York: Doubleday & McClure Co., 1899.
God's Puppets. New York: Macmillan Co., 1916.
In Our Town. New York: McClure, Phillips & Co., 1906.
In the Heart of a Fool. New York: Macmillan Co., 1918.
The Martial Adventures of Henry and Me. New York: Macmillan Co., 1918.
The Real Issue: A Book of Kansas Stories. Chicago: Way & Williams, 1896.
Stratagems and Spoils: Stories of Love and Politics. New York: Charles Scribner's Sons, 1901.

3. Editorials

The Editor and His People: Editorials by William Allen White, Selected

from the Emporia Gazette. Edited by Helen Ogden Mahin. New York: Macmillan Co., 1924.
Forty Years on Main Street. Edited by Russell H. Fitzgibbon. New York: Farrar & Rinehart, 1937.

4. Biography
The Autobiography of William Allen White. New York: Macmillan Co., 1946.
Calvin Coolidge, The Man Who Is President. New York: Macmillan Co., 1925.
Masks in a Pageant. New York: Macmillan Co., 1928.
A Puritan in Babylon: The Story of Calvin Coolidge. New York: Macmillan Co., 1938.
Woodrow Wilson, The Man, His Times, and His Task. Boston: Houghton Mifflin Co., 1924.

5. Political and Social Commentary
Boys—Then and Now. New York: Macmillan Co., 1926.
The Changing West: An Economic Theory About Our Golden Age. New York: Macmillan Co., 1939.
The Old Order Changeth: A View of American Democracy. New York: Macmillan Co., 1910.
Politics: The Citizen's Business. New York: Macmillan Co., 1924.
Some Cycles of Cathay. Chapel Hill: University of North Carolina Press, 1925.
A Theory of Spiritual Progress: An Address Delivered before the Phi Beta Kappa Society of Columbia University in the City of New York. Emporia: Gazette Press, 1910.
What It's All About: Being a Reporter's Story of the Early Campaign of 1936. New York: Macmillan Co., 1936.

6. Letters
Selected Letters of William Allen White, 1899–1943. Edited by Walter Johnson. New York: Henry Holt and Co., 1947.
Letters of William Allen White and a Young Man. Edited by Gil Wilson. New York: John Day Co., 1948.

7. Verse
Rhymes By Two Friends. Fort Scott, Kans.: M. L. Izor & Sons, 1893. In collaboration with Albert Bigelow Paine.

SECONDARY SOURCES

Bader, Robert S. *The Great Kansas Bond Scandal.* Lawrence: University Press of Kansas, 1982. Well-documented, dramatically written account of the Finney bank and bond scandal. Many references to the Whites.

Cless, G. H., Jr. "William Allen White's Reign of Terror." *Scribner's Commentator* 9 (December 1940):38–43. Representative example of personal attack on White by a reactionary isolationist.

Clough, Frank C. *William Allen White of Emporia.* New York: McGraw-Hill Book Co., 1941. Slight, eulogistic biography written near end of White's life by a long-time *Gazette* employee.

Clugston, William G. *Rascals in Democracy.* New York: Richard R. Smith, 1940. Contains chapter attacking White's liberalism. Intemperate but provocative diatribe by an opposition Kansas political reporter.

Davis, Kenneth S. "The Sage of Emporia." *American Heritage* 30 (October–November 1979):81–97. Illustrated critique of White's career.

Dubbert, Joe L. "William Allen White: Reflections on an American Life." *Markham Review* 4 (May 1974):41–47. Interesting survey of White's career as a progressive.

Elkins, William R. "William Allen White's Early Fiction," *Heritage of Kansas* 8 (1975):5–17. Analysis of some of the early short stories, especially those in *The Real Issue.*

Groman, George L. "W. A. White's Political Fiction: A Study in Emerging Progressivism." *Midwest Quarterly* 8 (October 1966):79–93. Analytical paraphrases of some of White's political fiction.

Hinshaw, David. *A Man From Kansas: The Story of William Allen White.* New York: G. P. Putnam's Sons, 1945. Reminiscent biography by a close friend and fellow Progressive Republican. Uncritical, often inaccurate.

Johnson, Walter. *The Battle against Isolation.* Chicago: University of Chicago Press, 1944. Documented study of moves to rally public support for FDR's foreign policy just prior to World War II, with emphasis on White.

———. *William Allen White's America.* New York: Henry Holt and Co., 1947. Definitive biography, admirably detailed and documented from primary sources.

Kraus, Joe W. "The Publication of William Allen White's *The Real Issue.*" *Kansas Historical Quarterly* 43 (Summer 1977):193–202. Publication history of White's first book of fiction.

La Forte, Robert S. *Leaders of Reform: Progressive Republicans in Kansas*

1900–1916. Lawrence: University Press of Kansas, 1974. Well-researched historical study with many references to White.

Ledner, Caryl. *Mary White*. New York: Bantam Books, 1977. The script, in "promotional novel" form, of the movie filmed for ABC Television by Rodnitz–Mattel Productions. A readable, sympathetic dramatization of Will White's personality. Compresses biographical details for dramatic effect, but not egregiously.

McKee, John DeWitt. *William Allen White: Maverick on Main Street*. Westport, Conn.: Greenwood Press, 1975. Analytical biography with focus on White's paradoxical public personality and political career.

Mangelsdorf, Philip. "When William Allen White and Ed Howe Covered the Republicans." *Journalism Quarterly* 3 (Autumn 1967):454–60. Discussion of contrasts in White's and Howe's coverages of 1896 Republican convention in St. Louis, based on files of Emporia *Gazette* and Atchinson *Globe*.

Mencken, H. L. "The Last of the Victorians." *Smart Set* 29 (October 1909):153–60. Most perceptive of contemporary reviews of White's fiction.

Resh, Richard W. "A Vision in Emporia: William Allen White's Search for Community." *Midcontinent American Studies Journal* 10 (Spring 1969):19–35. Intelligently critical, well-researched and written analysis of White's attempts to find spiritual values in a materialistic age.

Rich, Everett. *William Allen White: The Man from Emporia*. New York: Farrar & Rinehart, 1941. Earliest of the three scholarly biographies. Thoroughly documented, well-written critical study.

Sergeant, Elizabeth S. "The Citizen of Emporia." *Century Magazine* 113 (January 1927):308–16. Contemporary sketch and shrewd critique by a journalist friend.

Trattner, Walter I. "William Allen White and World War I." *Midwest Quarterly* 3 (January 1962):133–47. Traces White's evolution from confused neutral to determined belligerent as typical of Midwestern progressives.

Traylor, Jack W. "William Allen White's 1924 Gubernatorial Campaign." *Kansas Historical Quarterly* 42 (Spring 1976):180–91. Circumstantial account of White's independent candidacy.

Tuttle, William M. "Aid-to-the-Allies Short-of-War Versus American Intervention, 1940: A Reappraisal of William Allen White's Leadership." *Journal of American History* 56 (March 1970):840–58. Thoroughly documented analysis of White's illogical unwillingness to advocate direct U.S. intervention on the side of the Allies at the end of 1940.

White, William L. "The Sage of Emporia." *Nieman Reports* 23 (March 1969):23–29. Revealing reminiscent speech given at the University of Kansas during ceremonies in honor of his father's centennial.

"William Allen White of Emporia: An American Institution is Seventy." *Life*, 28 February 1938, pp. 9–13. Interesting photo-feature of White at age seventy.

Index